TODAY WI

Vo

Clifford Hill

The Centre for Biblical and Hebraic Studies

Copyright © The Centre for Biblical and Hebraic Studies 1999

Published by
The Centre for Biblical and Hebraic Studies,
a ministry of PWM Trust (Charity Number 326533)

First published 1999

All rights reserved.
No part of this publication may be reproduced or transmitted in any form or by any means, electronic or mechanical, including photocopy, recording, or any information storage and retrieval system,without permission in writing from the publisher.

Unless otherwise indicated, biblical quotes are from the
New International Version © 1973, 1978, 1984
by the International Bible Society.

ISBN: 1-872395-55-4

British Library Cataloguing in Publication Data.
A catalogue record for this book is available from the British Library.

Printed by Cox and Wyman, Reading, England

Manuscript typed by Jean Wolton and Ruth Addington

Typeset by Andrew Lewis

FOREWORD

There is an urgent need to recover the prophetic dimension in the life of the church and also at the heart of our national life. 'The Church', as Dr Philip Potter of South Africa once remarked, 'is the prophetic conscience of the nation'. In this defining moment in world history, one question cries out for an answer: 'Is there any word from the Lord?'.

Few people have done more to recover that truly prophetic note and apply it rigorously to our national life than Clifford Hill. Through his books, the magazine *Prophecy Today*, his involvement with government and a wide teaching ministry, the living word of scripture has again and again spoken like today's newspaper to an appreciative audience that literally spans the world. That is why I believe this book on the prophet Jeremiah is so timely.

Here in an accessible format for every concerned Christian is a clear exposition of the main features of Jeremiah's teaching. In plain terms, these pages help us understand the message and apply it to today's world.

The casual reader of scripture will wonder why Jeremiah is so important for us today. Firstly, we can all identify with someone like Jeremiah. From the moment of his call as a teenager to the time of his passing into obscurity (perhaps by stoning, according to tradition), he is a man who is overwhelmed by personal inadequacies and racked by a sense of unfitness for the task in hand.

We know these intimate, autobiographical details because, significantly, more is known of the life of Jeremiah than any of the other Old Testament prophets. As Alexander Stewart, the great Scottish expositor, once commented, Jeremiah is 'one of the most living books in the Bible, nonetheless divine because it is so intensely human'.

Secondly, the book of Jeremiah is one of the most neglected portions of scripture. Running to 51 chapters in all, here is a classic of 'War and Peace' proportions of which most Christians are largely ignorant.

The times in which Jeremiah lived are so like our own. Wars and rumours of wars, rapid constitutional change, violence in the streets and sleaze in high places – all these called for the most extraordinary courage from a timid youth whose tremendous destiny it was to declare judgment and, through judgment, bring hope to his nation in one of the most testing hours in the history of God's people.

'What is needed today', an elderly Christian man said to me, 'is a God-communicating word from heaven'. That is the prophetic heartbeat so characteristic of Clifford's life and ministry which I have come, along with many others, to value highly. It throbs through these challenging pages from start to finish.

So as we blow the dust off these neglected pages of Jeremiah and open ourselves to what God has to say to us today, we should make the prayer of Samuel our own prayer: 'Speak Lord, for your servant is listening'.

Rev David JB Anderson
General Secretary
Evangelical Alliance Scotland

PREFACE

The Book of Jeremiah

The Book of Jeremiah, as we have it in our Bibles, is one of the major books of the writing prophets of Israel. It is a unique collection of sayings of one of the most influential and outstanding of Israel's prophets.

Jeremiah was the founder of a school of prophets, although he probably didn't know it. For most of his life he appears to have been a lonely figure with his only companion being the faithful Baruch who wrote down the words that the prophet received from the Lord.

It was probably only after Jeremiah had died that the school of prophets bearing his name grew. Baruch may have been influential in this gathering and preserving of his masters sayings so that they could survive the turbulent times of the sixth century BC. How they were edited and brought together in their present form, no-one knows, but they were passed down into the great prophetic literature of Israel which, sometime during the Second Temple Period, was collected into the Hebrew Bible.

Historical Background to Jeremiah's Ministry

The beginning of Chapter 1 tells us that Jeremiah's ministry started during the reign of Josiah. We know that Jeremiah's ministry lasted at least 40 years but the grey areas of dating are the beginning and the end. His own testimony tells us that he was a young man; in fact he described himself as 'only a child' (1: 7). It is quite likely that he was a teenager when he experienced his call to the prophetic ministry. In 621 BC, Josiah initiated a programme of major repairs to the Temple, during which the 'Book of the Law' was discovered which most scholars believe to be a section, at least, of Deuteronomy. This had considerable influence upon the religious reforms Josiah carried out and the formal renewal of the covenant. These events, followed shortly after by the untimely death of Josiah at Megiddo in an unnecessary clash with Egypt, had a profound effect upon the young prophet.

As far as we are aware, Jeremiah's ministry was almost totally confined to Jerusalem and its environs. His home town of Anathoth was only two or three miles north of Jerusalem. Today it is part of the suburbs of the city. Jeremiah came from a long line of priestly families who traced their ancestry back to Abiathar who was Chief Priest in David's time but was deposed by Solomon (1 Kings 2: 26). Abiathar himself was of the lineage of Eli the priest of Shiloh who nurtured the boy Samuel. It must have been a great shock to Jeremiah's proud priestly family to discover that they had raised a prophet instead of a priest!

Jeremiah lived through the most dramatic period in the history of Israel prior to the period covered by the New Testament. He saw the reigns of Josiah, Jehoiahaz, Jehoiakim, Jehoiachin and Zedekiah, the last five Kings of Judah. Jerusalem surrendered three times during his ministry: once to Egypt after the death of Josiah when they deposed Jehoiahaz and set Jehoiakim on the throne; and twice to the Babylonians. In the first of these (596 BC) Jehoiachin was deposed and Zedekiah was made king.

Zedekiah reigned eleven years and, in 586 BC, when the city was sacked and burned, Zedekiah's eyes were gouged out after he had witnessed the slaughter of his family. He was taken in chains together with thousands of his countrymen to Babylon. Soon after, there was yet another minor revolt in which Babylonian officials were murdered. A remnant decided, much against Jeremiah's counsel, to flee to Egypt and they forcibly took the prophet with them. This is the last recorded event in Jeremiah's eventful life.

Personality of the Prophet

Jeremiah had a highly sensitive nature and entered fully into the experience of the changing fortunes of the nation. He was a great patriot, loving his nation and personally identifying with its changing fortunes. He felt the sins of the people as though they were his own, taking upon himself the enormous burden of intercession for the people before God. It was a rebellious generation, addicted to idolatry and unprincipled, both in personal and social morality.

The book of Jeremiah gives fascinating glimpses into the prophet's personal life. Many times he bares his soul as he cries out to the Lord in anguish for what he sees in the nation and what he knows to be the inevitable consequences of the wickedness he sees all around him. Passages like, 'Oh, my anguish, my anguish! I writhe in pain. Oh, the agony of my heart! My heart pounds within me, I cannot keep silent' (4: 19), show the tremendous suffering of the prophet. His distress was intense because he was permitted to foresee the coming tragedy in the life of the nation and yet he was powerless to change the situation. His message was ignored and he was despised and rejected by the nation. There are many similarities between Jeremiah's ministry and that of Jesus, both in their treatment by the authorities and in the message they bore.

The Message

The four major elements in the message that Jeremiah proclaimed were: Warnings; Repentance; Trust; and Hope.

Jeremiah's message has often been characterised as one of doom and gloom. That is far from the truth. Certainly, he lived through terrible times and he gave clear warnings of the consequences of the policies of the rulers and the lifestyle of the people. Jeremiah was proved to be perfectly right in the warnings that he gave to the nation. If his counsel had been heeded and the nation had put their trust in the Lord instead of in pacts and treaties with foreign nations, the subsequent history of the nation would have been very different.

Despite the widespread rejection of the warnings he brought, Jeremiah's message was one of hope for the future. Long before the actual destruction of Jerusalem, which he eventually came to see as inevitable, he was focusing upon the time of restoration, the joyous return of the exiles and the establishment of a New Covenant through which every believer would have a personal relationship with God.

Relevance for Today

There are so many similarities between the situation Jeremiah faced and conditions in the world today which underline the relevance of his message. The biblical witness to the nature of God is that he is unchanging from one generation to the next. Therefore, what he said to his servants the prophets under similar circumstances he will be saying to his people today. This underlines the practical usefulness of a study of the ministry of Jeremiah for today. The six sins of Jerusalem that Jeremiah pinpointed in his famous 'Temple Sermon' (Chapter 7) can all be seen in our national life today. We need to hear what God said to his people then.

On the international scene there is the ever-increasing threat of war, international terrorism and violence on an unprecedented scale. Jeremiah's answer to all these problems was a clear trumpet call to faith in God as the only hope for the nations. If we are to avoid an international version of the kind of Babylonian Holocaust which submerged that whole region in bloodshed, the message of Jeremiah needs to be heard in our world today.

About this Book

The purpose of this book is to bring the message of Jeremiah alive for today. It is part commentary, part exegesis and part devotional. I have sought to use the best available scholarship in the studies while at the same time avoiding the use of technical language. I hope the result is a very readable explanation of each passage and how it may speak to us today.

The front cover with its picture of a potter at work is in reference to the account in Chapter 18 of Jeremiah's visit to the potter's shop. There he watched the man at work and, as he did so, God gave him a message that was not only relevant to Israel in his own day, but was a promise of blessing addressed to all nations for all time.

These studies in the prophecies of Jeremiah have been arranged in the form of daily readings, with an explanation of the text and the application of the message in the form of a thought for the day, followed by a short prayer. I trust they will be of help to many who are seeking to hear from God and to receive guidance for their own lives. I trust also that some measure of the rich maturity of faith of one of the great prophets of Israel will be conveyed to God's people today.

This volume deals with the first half of the book of Jeremiah and is the first in a series that will eventually cover all the writing prophets.

Clifford Hill
July 1999

Today with Jeremiah

KNOWN IN THE WOMB

Jeremiah 1: 4-5
The word of the Lord came to me, saying, 'Before I formed you in the womb I knew you, before you were born I set you apart; I appointed you as a prophet to the nations'.

Comment

This is an important verse which lays the foundation for Jeremiah's ministry. In the phrase 'the word of the Lord came to me', the Hebrew word translated by the verb 'came' can mean 'appeared', or 'came into being'. This indicates the way in which the prophet received the word of God. He did not work it out in his mind by his own wisdom. God planted his word into his mind. It was 'birthed' within him through the Spirit of God speaking into his spirit and creating his thoughts.

The phrase 'before I formed you in the womb', means that God actually watched over Jeremiah's conception. From that moment, before his tiny body began to take shape within the womb of his mother, God was planning to use him as a prophet to the nation. From the moment of conception God was moulding the character of the prophet, preparing him for the most difficult and exacting ministry of any of the prophets of the Old Testament. Before he was born, Jeremiah was set apart for his special calling to convey the word of God to the nation. While still in the womb, God appointed him to be his prophet, and mouthpiece to the people.

Like the prophet Samuel, whose mother gave him to the Lord while he was still in her womb, Jeremiah must also have had a special mother. We know nothing about her except that she was the wife of a priest, a descendant of Zadok and Abiathar, whose family home was in Anathoth, just north of Jerusalem (1 Kings 2: 26). Today Anathoth is a suburb of modern Jerusalem.

The reason why God chose Jeremiah from the moment of conception and watched over his development through the pre-birth period of character formation, was because he was called to carry the word of God at the most critical time of Israel's history since they entered the land under Joshua. The very survival of the nation and the great city of Jerusalem was going to depend upon the response to the message Jeremiah carried. He was destined to meet fierce opposition. Would he be strong enough for the task? God took care to watch over his chosen prophet from the moment of his conception in the womb.

Clearly that pre-birth period is of great importance for character formation. Yet millions of healthy babies are cruelly aborted every year by our godless generation. Who knows how many of these babies would have been destined for great things? A wicked generation throws away the precious gift of life – unwanted, unloved and uncared-for. But God knows each one from the moment of conception. He is the Creator of all things and he alone can create life. In some amazing way that defies human logic, God actually knows each one and loves each one of his children. He loves them enough for Christ to die for them.

Prayer
Father, forgive us that we are so careless with your precious gift of life. Help me to understand the significance of this message for me and for my family.

DO NOT BE AFRAID

Jeremiah 1: 6-8
'Ah, Sovereign Lord', I said, 'I do not know how to speak; I am only a child'. But the Lord said to me, 'Do not say, "I am only a child". You must go to everyone I send you to and say whatever I command you. Do not be afraid of them, for I am with you and will rescue you', declares the Lord.

Comment

In yesterday's reading we saw how God watched over the young Jeremiah from the moment of conception. The preparation of the prophet continued through infancy and childhood. As the son of a priest he would have been schooled for the priesthood. An important part of this would have been learning the Torah – the teaching that God gave to Moses. He would also have been taught the history of the nation from the standpoint of God's dealing with his covenant people.

Jeremiah's training for the priesthood was part of God's intention for the prophet. But his family did not know that they were training a prophet, not a priest! That would have been anathema to them! In later years, as his ministry developed, Jeremiah's family became bitter opponents and caused him much suffering.

It was probably not until he was a young man that Jeremiah himself became aware that he would not be undertaking the duties of a priest. He would not be taking his tour of duty in the Temple. He was destined to preach outside the Temple, not in it! In his adult life he would be in constant contention with the Temple priests and prophets.

Jeremiah's response to the Lord when he first heard him speak directly to him, calling him to the ministry of the prophet, was to protest that he was too young. 'I am only a child', he said. He was probably in his late teens or early twenties. But in an age-dominated society that was a mere child, especially for the task for which God was calling him.

He was immediately rebuked, 'Do not say, "I am only a child". You must go to everyone I send you to and say whatever I command you.' Then came the promise upon which Jeremiah was to rely for the rest of his life, 'Do not be afraid of them, for I am with you and will rescue you'.

There would be many times in the prophet's life when that promise would be put to the test as Jeremiah faced an angry mob, or outraged priests, or cruel kings. But the God who had watched over his earliest character formation kept his word and although there would be many times when Jeremiah's faith would be severely tested, the strength of the Lord was always sufficient for him.

When God calls us to serve him he always equips us. He never gives us a task without also giving the enabling.

Prayer
Thank you, Father, that you always keep your promises. May your strength be sufficient for all you want me to accomplish this day.

UPROOTING AND PLANTING

Jeremiah 1: 9-10
Then the Lord reached out his hand and touched my mouth and said to me, 'Now, I have put my words in your mouth. See, today I appoint you over nations and kingdoms to uproot and tear down, to destroy and overthrow, to build and to plant.'

Comment

Yesterday we saw Jeremiah's reaction to the word he received from God, appointing him to the ministry of the prophecy. His immediate thought was one of personal inadequacy. The Lord, who had read his thoughts as well as heard his words, knew that it was not just his youthfulness that troubled the young Jeremiah.

It may well be that, like Isaiah, Jeremiah also felt unworthy to undertake a ministry which demanded that he should be the mouthpiece of the Lord. As a prophet he would have to declare the words of the living God. It was an awesome task.

Isaiah had cried out, 'Woe is me for I am a man of unclean lips'. Jeremiah's thoughts were probably very similar, because God touched his mouth in much the same way as he had touched Isaiah and pronounced him clean.

For Jeremiah the experience was accompanied by the promise that God had put his words in his mouth. This was immediately followed by God's own description of the task to which he was calling the prophet. It was given in the form of a divine command: 'I appoint you over nations and kingdoms, to uproot and tear down, to destroy and overthrow, to build and to plant.'

There are six verbs in the task Jeremiah was given. They are in three pairs; four were negative and two were positive. Four were to oppose and pull down the existing institutions and two were to create new things.

From the start, Jeremiah knew that his was to be an unpopular task which would bring him into great conflict with the authorities and rulers, both religious and secular. It was a daunting task from which a lesser mortal would have shrunk. But God had been preparing this young man for ministry since the moment of his conception.

If God calls us to a difficult task, or puts us into a seemingly impossible situation to serve him, we can be sure that his preparation will have been adequate for the task. He never leaves us to serve him in our own strength. The most important thing is for us to know that we are where the Lord wants us to be. If we are in the centre of his will, however difficult the situation, he will uphold us, strengthen and guide us. If God gives a task he always gives the enabling.

Prayer
Lord, forgive me if I am sometimes fearful. Help me to have confidence, not in my own ability and strength, but in your good plans for my life.

THE ALMOND TREE

Jeremiah 1: 11-12
The word of the Lord came to me: 'What do you see, Jeremiah?' 'I see the branch of an almond tree', I replied. The Lord said to me, 'You have seen correctly, for I am watching to see that my word is fulfilled'.

Comment

This is Jeremiah's first prophecy and it was important for him as a confirmation that he was rightly hearing from the Lord. After the question, 'What do you see?' and Jeremiah's response, God said, 'You have seen correctly'. That confirmed to the young prophet that he was rightly perceiving what God wanted him to observe. This was going to be of great importance in future for the kind of ministry Jeremiah was to carry out.

Some scholars think that when Jeremiah said, 'I see the branch of an almond tree', he was seeing a vision, rather than a real almond tree. But this is to misunderstand the whole basis of Jeremiah's ministry. He was not a visionary like Ezekiel. His task was that of the watchman, observing what was happening around him; then, under the direction of the Spirit of God, rightly interpreting the significance of what he saw.

Many times Jeremiah was told to go and look at something: look up and down the streets of Jerusalem (5: 1); stand at the cross-roads and look (6: 16); go and watch the potter at work (18: 1). So this first 'practice exercise' was of great importance.

Jeremiah immediately perceived the significance of the almond tree, traditionally the first tree to bloom after the winter in Israel. As he pronounced 'almond tree' in

Hebrew, it would have reminded him of the word for 'watching'. The significance of the pun was not lost on Jeremiah. He possibly spoke the word aloud in responding to the Lord's question. In reply, God confirmed that this interpretation was correct. He was indeed watching over his word to see that it was fulfilled.

From that moment, Jeremiah knew that, provided he was faithful, keeping himself in a right relationship with the Lord, he could rely absolutely upon God to fulfil his word. If God told him to make a particular pronouncement, Jeremiah could do so, knowing that he was speaking the truth and that God would accomplish whatever he promised or pronounced.

The outstanding thing which we learn from the prophets is that God is faithful. He is consistent. He does not say something today and deny it the next day. If he declares something good, it will always be good; evil will always be evil. However much we may be let down by human friends and loved ones, God will never let us down. He is faithful under all circumstances.

Prayer
Teach me, Lord, more of your nature. Help me to know your faithfulness that I may never doubt you. Increase my trust day by day.

IN THE DESERT

Jeremiah 2: 1-3
The word of the Lord came to me: 'Go and proclaim in the hearing of Jerusalem: "I remember the devotion of your youth, how as a bride you loved me and followed me through the desert, through a land not sown. Israel was holy to the Lord, the firstfruits of his harvest; all who devoured her were held guilty, and disaster overtook them"', declares the Lord.

Comment

There is a certain pathos about this first public message that Jeremiah was given to declare. The message from the Lord is one of nostalgia, looking back to the days between the exodus from Egypt and the entry into the promised land. Those were the days when Israel dwelt in tents. They were a nomadic people with no settled homeland.

For most of that forty year period Israel travelled through the desert. It was an exacting time for the tribal leaders and a time of enormous strain for Moses in maintaining order, discipline and unity among the tribes. But historically it was the time when the tribes became a nation. Their shared experience of facing the dangers and privation of the wilderness welded them together.

Above all, the sojourn in the desert was a spiritual experience that established them as a covenant people under God. They were his bride, newly brought into a sweet covenant relationship with him. 'Israel was holy to the Lord'. This means that they were separated from the world, from the flesh-pots of Egypt, and the influence of pagan gods. They were in an exclusive relationship with the Lord.

The fruit of that relationship was that God provided for his people in what would otherwise have been hopeless situations from which they would not have survived. He provided food and water. He provided protection and care for them.

Jeremiah thus began his ministry by reminding the people of God's great act of saving them from slavery and his loving provision for them through the desert. For Jeremiah, and for all the prophets, the desert was not a place of separation from God. It was a place of separation from the world. It was a place where there were no distractions, no worldly attractions to compete for their attention.

The great silence of the desert was filled with the presence of the living God. It was here that Israel learned to love the Lord and to trust him. In this first message given to Jeremiah, God remembers the devotion of Israel's youth, her dependence upon him and her love.

How easy it is to lose the simple love and trust we had when we first opened our heart to the Lord.

Prayer
Lord, help me to regain my first love, even if it means taking me back through the desert. I can only do this as you go with me.

Today with Jeremiah

WORTHLESS IDOLS

Jeremiah 2: 5-6
This is what the Lord says: 'What fault did your fathers find in me, that they strayed so far from me? They followed worthless idols and became worthless themselves. They did not ask, "Where is the Lord, who brought us up out of Egypt and led us up out of the barren wilderness, through a land of deserts and rifts, a land of drought and darkness, a land where no-one travels and no-one lives?"'

Comment

There is further pathos in our reading today which reveals something of the heart of God. His question, 'What fault did your fathers find in me?' shows the suffering in God's heart when his people are faithless and turn away from him. It is as though God is saying, 'After all I have done for you, how could you possibly deny me and turn your back upon me?'

It is almost inconceivable in human relationships that someone would turn against you if your whole life was devoted to serving them. But yes, it does happen! The sense of rejection and personal suffering under such circumstances gives intense pain. The more we have given to our friend or loved one before the break in relationship, the more intense our pain. Sometimes the pain is accompanied by a sense of great injustice. 'What wrong have I done?' we ask. 'Why am I being treated in this way?' 'What more could I have done?'

This is what God was saying to Jeremiah. It was not just the young people who had strayed from God, but their fathers, the leaders of the nation, had turned away from him. They had forgotten all that God had done for them in former generations. They had turned their backs on the God who had rescued their forefathers from Egypt and who had cared for them through the long years in the desert. All that God had done for them was now forgotten, or discarded as of no value. Now they had compounded their offence by turning to idols. The idols were worthless, and in worshipping them the people of God had become worthless to him.

That does not mean that as individuals the people were worthless. God would not make such a statement. All are sinners, and God so loved the world that Christ was willing to die for sinful men and women. What this statement 'they became worthless themselves' means is that they were no longer able to carry out the purposes of God as his covenant people.

This is a warning to us all. If we are unfaithful and turn away from God, he cannot use us to fulfil his purposes. We become useless to him as his servants. No, he will never reject us and we are always of infinite worth to him as his children, but we can frustrate his good plans for us so that he is unable to use us as he wishes.

Prayer
Father, how glad we are that our lives are in your hands! Make me more sensitive to the promptings of your Holy Spirit so that I am aware of the dangers of drifting away from the centre of your will for my life.

FAITHFULNESS

Jeremiah 2: 11-12
'Has a nation ever changed its gods? (Yet they are not gods at all.) But my people have exchanged their Glory for worthless idols. Be appalled at this, O heavens, and shudder with great horror', declares the Lord.

Comment

Something of the Lord's indignation is expressed in this passage. Justice is outraged! The most appaling thing imaginable has happened. You could travel from Cyprus to the Arabian Gulf and you would not find a parallel. Nothing like it has ever been seen before; a nation has changed its gods!

Even more incredible was the fact that the nation that had done this was the only nation to have known the one true and only God! Jeremiah saw all the heavens appalled and shuddering with horror. It was just unbelievable that this could have happened. Even the pagan nations, with their worthless idols of wood and stone, remained faithful to their gods. Yet here was Israel, a nation chosen by the God of the whole universe as his own special people, wilfully and recklessly discarding their God.

The effect of what Israel had done was to exchange their Glory for worthless idols. The idolatry in Jeremiah's time was everywhere to be seen: in the countryside, with altars to pagan gods on the high places of every hilltop and mountain; in the villages, with their Asherah poles; in the walled cities, with their street-corner shrines; and even in the holy city of Jerusalem, with altars to foreign gods within sight of the Temple itself.

In Jerusalem people openly worshipped at the street-corner shrines especially at the time of the spring fertility festival. They baked cakes with the image of Astarte, the Babylonian goddess known as 'the Queen of Heaven' (7: 18). They offered worship to her because they thought she was responsible for the power of the Babylonian armies which were conquering nation after nation. Instead of putting their trust in the Lord their God, as Jeremiah urged, they changed and ran after foreign idols.

Amazing as this may seem, in the highly secularised world of today, we often do the same. We worship our technology, our computers, gadgets, domestic appliances, cars, houses and all the material wealth we are able to obtain. We have exchanged the God and Father of our Lord Jesus Christ who has been worshipped in the land for nearly two thousand years, not for the gods of wood and stone of the ancient world, but for the gods of metal and plastic of the modern world.

Just stop to think which of all your possessions are essential for life. You will be surprised how much you could do without! After all, what is the purpose of life? What are you striving to achieve? What are you hoping will remain after your death as a fitting memorial to your life? Will it be said that you exchanged the Lord your God for worthless idols?

Prayer
O Father, help me to love you more and to be faithful to you. Guard me against following the values of the world, and striving after worthless idols.

BROKEN CISTERNS

Jeremiah 2: 13
'My people have committed two sins: they have forsaken me, the spring of living water, and have dug their own cisterns, broken cisterns that cannot hold water.'

Comment

Water was very important in Israel – in fact it still is! Without water there could be no life. If the spring and autumn rains did not fall on the land to water the ground and bring life to the seed, there would be no harvest. Drought was one of the most feared enemies in the Middle East, especially among simple farming communities.

The Bedouin tribesmen with their sheep and goats were dependent upon travelling from one water-hole to the next. If they reached a watering place where the spring had dried up it could spell disaster for both animals and humans.

The nation of Israel had once been an itinerant people and the account of their travels in the wilderness was passed down from generation to generation. Since the settlement in the land of Canaan, in every village, the well was a place of great social importance. Without it life could not be sustained.

Fresh running water, living water, became a symbol of life for the prophets. The springs around Mount Hermon were well known for the pure fresh water that bubbled up through the rocky ground and fed the Sea of Galilee, eventually flowing into the Jordan. They were dependable springs that, even in a time of drought, never ran dry. For the prophets they became symbols of the faithfulness of God who never ceased to love and care for his people.

Fresh water was just as important for city-dwellers. A constant supply was essential at all times and especially in a time of war when foreign armies laid siege around the city walls. This was why King Hezekiah had diverted the Gihon stream and secured water for the city. But many households also dug their own cisterns to collect rainwater and to keep it cool and fresh even during the hot summer days. But cistern-stored water never tasted as good or as fresh as water from the stream or from a running spring.

Jeremiah likened God to a spring of fresh living water from which people had refused to drink, preferring stale lukewarm water from their own cisterns. How could they be so foolish? But how many times do we do the same kind of thing, preferring our own wisdom, or the counsel of other human beings, to the help of the living God? He is, as Jesus said, 'a spring of water welling up to eternal life'.

Jesus promised 'whoever drinks the water I give him will never thirst' (John 4: 14). That is a wonderful promise of which we can avail ourselves today.

Prayer
Lord Jesus, enable me, this day, to drink deeply from the spring of water that you so freely supply to all those who love and trust you.

Today with Jeremiah

UNFAITHFULNESS

Jeremiah 2: 17-19
'Have you not brought this on yourselves by forsaking the Lord your God when he led you in the way? Now why go to Egypt to drink water from the Shihor? And why go to Assyria to drink water from the River? Your wickedness will punish you; your backsliding will rebuke you. Consider then and realise how evil and bitter it is for you when you forsake the Lord your God and have no awe of me', declares the Lord, the Lord Almighty.

Comment

Jeremiah lived in a time of international turbulence. The two great military powers were Babylon in the east and Egypt in the west. Judah was one of the last independent states not to have been crushed by either of the great powers. The air was full of political intrigue. Among the king's advisers in Jerusalem there were those who were pro-Egypt and who advocated making a treaty with the Egyptians. There were others who advised sending emissaries to Assyria to try to stir up a revolt within the Babylonian Empire.

Jeremiah poured scorn on both options. His counsel was quite simple – put your trust in the Lord and do not enter any political alliances with foreign states.

'Why go to Egypt?' he asked. They were more unreliable and would certainly forsake the tiny insignificant nation of Judah if they perceived it to be in their own best interests to do so. 'Why go to Assyria?' he asked. That would be a dangerous game to play and if such an intrigue were exposed it would certainly bring down the wrath of Babylon upon tiny Judah.

'You have brought all this trouble upon yourselves', was Jeremiah's message. They had done this by forsaking the Lord. He was the only one who could be trusted fully and completely. 'Consider then and realise how evil and bitter it is for you when you forsake the Lord'. He was their God, but they had no respect for him. There was no 'awe' of the Lord among the people.

Even though everything was going wrong in the nation and they could see no clear way forward, they were still not prepared to put their trust in God. They could only think of more devious ways of making pacts and treaties with human institutions.

How often we do the same! When everything goes wrong we say, 'There is nothing else to do except to pray!' But shouldn't prayer come first? Why is it the last resort? Why do we look for every human solution before we turn to the Lord for help? Are we not just as foolish as the people of Judah in Jeremiah's day?

Prayer
Lord, help me to put you first in my life; to seek you and your way, first and foremost.

COME AND SAVE US!

Jeremiah 2: 26-27
'As a thief is disgraced when he is caught, so the house of Israel is disgraced – they, their kings and their officials, their priests and their prophets. They say to wood, "You are my father", and to stone, "You gave me birth". They have turned their backs to me and not their faces; yet when they are in trouble, they say, "Come and save us!"'

Comment

Jeremiah could never cease to be amazed that the whole nation of Israel was involved in idolatry. If any people had cause to be grateful and to remain faithful to God it was Israel, with their heritage of God's amazing deeds on their behalf.

From the time of Moses it had been incumbent upon parents to teach their children the history of the nation, and the terms of the covenant. This had no doubt been neglected for a long time. At the same time, worship at the Temple had become increasingly formal and remote from the people.

In our reading today, Jeremiah complains that the whole nation, including both secular and religious leaders, were practising idolatry. They had idols of wood and stone to whom they ascribed the power even to give life itself!

The greatest anomaly was that when they were in trouble they turned back to the God of their fathers and cried out, 'Come and save us!' To Jeremiah this was the height of hypocrisy. They ignored God all the time everything was going well with them.

In times of peace and prosperity they turned their backs upon God and joined in all the exciting festivals and pagan partying of the Canaanites and their other unbelieving neighbours. They entered wholeheartedly into the orgies of self-indulgence, sexual excesses, feasts and revelries which were part of the religious practices against which Israel had been warned from the time of Moses.

Suddenly, however, there was a change of mood among the people. The land was under imminent threat of invasion from the all-conquering Babylonian armies. There was widespread panic; priests and people alike were crying out to God to come and save them! The prophet Jeremiah was not impressed. In fact, he was outraged!

But don't we do the same today? There were national days of prayer during the Second World War. There was great acknowledgment of God. Many people went to church, but as times of peace and prosperity increased, the nation turned its back upon the God of our fathers.

We do the same in our personal lives. We often neglect prayer and forget God until some family crisis or personal problem arises. Then we cry out to God, 'Come and save us!'

Prayer
Forgive me, Father, for my lack of constancy and commitment. Draw me closer to you this very day.

Today with Jeremiah

THE FORGETFUL BRIDE

Jeremiah 2: 32 and 34-35
'Does a maiden forget her jewellery, a bride her wedding ornaments? Yet my people have forgotten me, days without number... On your clothes men find the lifeblood of the innocent poor, though you did not catch them breaking in. Yet in spite of all this you say, "I am innocent; he is not angry with me". But I will pass judgment on you because you say, "I have not sinned".'

Comment

In our reading today Jeremiah uses the striking illustration of a bride going to her wedding and forgetting to dress in her gown and bridal paraphernalia. It is, of course, unthinkable! He intended it to make that kind of impact. The bride, in preparing for the happiest day of her life so far, would be keen to take care of every detail so that she would look her best for the great occasion.

Jeremiah used the very 'unthinkableness' of such a situation to provide a comparison with Israel forgetting God. They have done so 'days without number' is the charge. In forgetting God they had neglected all the standards of righteousness. The nation was full of idolatry, injustice and immorality. All this was the result of turning away from God and neglecting the Torah. Yet, despite all this wickedness in the nation, they still protested their innocence.

This was the greatest offence. There was no recognition of wrong-doing. The whole nation – people, priests and leaders – was so secularised, so far from God and so spiritually dead, that they could not even recognise their own sinfulness. This caused them not to recognise the signs of the times. God had sent them many warning signs and had allowed many things to happen which should have been warnings to them that something was badly wrong in their national life. But they were insensitive to such warnings. They simply protested their innocence and that God was not angry with them. It was this attitude that was the real cause of judgment coming upon them.

God loves to show his mercy and forgiveness to his people. This is a major expression of his love. We only have to confess our wrong-doing and he is quick to forgive us and to restore us to a close relationship with him. But if we harden our hearts and say there is nothing wrong, if we say that we have not sinned or in any way offended God, we cannot expect forgiveness.

How the Lord longs for us to come to him in penitence and in simple trust so that he can enfold us in his fatherly love and protection.

Prayer
Lord, I acknowledge that I do wrong in so many ways. Forgive me my proneness to sin and my vain attempts to hide it.

THE SPRING RAINS

Jeremiah 3: 2-3a
'Look up to the barren heights and see. Is there any place where you have not been ravished? By the roadside you sat waiting for lovers, sat like a nomad in the desert. You have defiled the land with your prostitution and wickedness. Therefore the showers have been withheld, and no spring rains have fallen.'

Comment

The prophets all used the term 'prostitution' to mean 'idolatry'. They saw running after other gods as a form of spiritual adultery. The reasoning behind this was that Israel had entered into a covenant with God which was equivalent to a marriage relationship. To forsake God and engage in intercourse with pagan gods was spiritual adultery. It was breaking the covenant vows taken by the nation.

In our reading today Jeremiah was thinking of the practices out in the countryside where the people of Israel and Judah joined in the celebrations of Canaanite festivities at the high places. Jeremiah saw the whole land as being defiled by the wickedness of the people. They had been breaking both the first and the second commandments (Exodus 20).

An essential part of the prophet's ministry was to watch what was happening in the nation and on the international scene. He was concerned with the moral and spiritual health of the nation and therefore took a lively interest in political as well as domestic affairs.

But the prophets also noted what was happening in the world of nature. They believed that the weather and all natural phenomena were directly under God's control. Therefore, when the spring rains failed, God had withheld them. It was the prophet's task to get before the Lord and find out why God was punishing the land and endangering the harvest on which people's lives depended.

This was a clear sign that something was wrong, but there was no response from the people. 'In vain I punished your people; they did not respond to correction' (Jeremiah 2: 30).

In our day, if the church were acting as the prophet to the nation we would be interpreting the signs relating to national events and to natural disasters.

Have we become so secularised that we cannot recognise the spiritual significance of events in the nation, or in the church, or in our own lives? Do we no longer believe in the activity of God in the world, or in our own lives? It is time to seek the Lord for understanding.

Prayer
Father, help me to be sensitive to your deeds, to understand and rightly interpret the warning signs as well as your blessings.

THE MERCY OF GOD

Jeremiah 3: 11-13
The Lord said to me, 'Faithless Israel is more righteous than unfaithful Judah. Go, proclaim this message towards the north: "Return, faithless Israel", declares the Lord, "I will frown on you no longer, for I am merciful", declares the Lord, "I will not be angry for ever. Only acknowledge your guilt – you have rebelled against the Lord your God, you have scattered your favours to foreign gods under every spreading tree, and have not obeyed me"', declares the Lord.

Comment

Jeremiah's ministry was based in Jerusalem. He was primarily a prophet to Judah, the southern kingdom. At the time of his call to the ministry God had said to him, 'See, today I appoint you over nations and kingdoms'. Thus, although his main responsibility was to bring the word of God to Judah, he was sometimes used to speak to other nations.

In our reading today, Jeremiah is told to go and proclaim a message to the northern kingdom, Israel. It is essential to remember that Israel had been overrun by the Assyrians one hundred years earlier. Samaria had been destroyed and much of the population had been taken as slaves to Nineveh, or settled in towns around the Assyrian empire.

The conquerors had also brought in communities from other captured nations and settled them in Israel. This was in order to mix the population and eliminate nationalist revolt. Thus began the mixed-race Samaritan people. They were regarded as 'aliens' by those of 'pure blood' in the tribe of Judah and by the Hebrew remnant in Israel.

Jeremiah knew what was happening and his call was specifically to the Hebrew people remaining in the land. If they would refrain from intermarriage and acknowledge their guilt – that they had rebelled against God – he would be gracious and merciful to them.

This prophecy that Jeremiah was sent to declare among the towns and villages of Israel, must surely have come as a wonderful message of love and mercy from God to the remnant of Israel. They must have felt lost and abandoned after the disaster to the land. Surely God had deserted them. They had no hope of redemption from the yoke of Assyria. But here was a beautiful word of hope.

God had not forgotten them. Although they had brought the tragedy upon themselves, God still loved them and was longing to bring them back into a close relationship with himself.

The Lord is always loving and gracious. However far we have strayed from him, he is never far from us. He never forgets us or forsakes us. Even in the midst of great trouble we have only to reach out. He is there, in an instant, beside us, comforting, forgiving and lovingly restoring us.

Prayer
Father, thank you for your unbreakable love. Help me to show my thankfulness throughout this day.

FAITHFUL REMNANT

Jeremiah 3: 14-15
'Return, faithless people,' declares the Lord, 'for I am your husband. I will choose you – one from a town and two from a clan – and bring you to Zion. Then I will give you shepherds after my own heart, who will lead you with knowledge and understanding.'

Comment

Today's reading follows the message to Israel that we considered yesterday. Despite the tragedy that had happened to Israel in being conquered by Assyria, God still loved and cared for the people. He knew that there was a remnant in the nation who remained faithful to him.

In times of national disaster the good, as well as the wicked, suffer. Our shared citizenship means that we are all affected by the national fortunes. But our spiritual life need not be determined by that of the nation as a whole. There is always a remnant who remain faithful to the Lord even in the hardest times.

When the nation suffers grave misfortune the faithful remnant are of great importance. They are the ones who are open to the word of God, who are listening to him, and they are the ones he can use to fulfil his purposes. Through them God wants to reach the whole nation to carry out his work of revival and restoration.

This is the message that Jeremiah carried to the shattered northern kingdom of Israel under the heel of the Assyrians. It was a call for the whole nation to return to him so that he would forgive them and restore them. But the call was directed to one or two in each town or community whom God could use as his faithful shepherds to the people. He laid upon them the responsibility to witness to others. But they were not left alone in this mission. The Lord himself had not abandoned them and was watching over them in love and tenderness.

There are many people today who are lonely in their spiritual pilgrimage, who do not enjoy good teaching or worship or fellowship in their local church. They sometimes feel that they are the only believers left, but God knows those who are faithful to him. They are part of the remnant of his people who, in the hardest times, he plans to use as his faithful shepherds.

Prayer
Lord, we praise you that you never forget. When we feel alone, reassure us with your word. Make me one of your faithful servants.

Today with Jeremiah

OUR FATHER

Jeremiah 3: 19
'I myself said, "How gladly would I treat you like sons and give you a desirable land, the most beautiful inheritance of any nation". I thought you would call me "Father" and not turn away from following me.'

Comment

This is one of the very few passages in the prophetic writings that refers explicitly to the Fatherhood of God. The best known such reference is in Isaiah's great Messianic prophecy concerning the coming of Messiah who, he says, will be called 'Wonderful Counsellor, Mighty God, Everlasting Father'.

In our reading today God says to Israel how gladly he would have treated them like sons. He did not want to judge them, or rebuke them, or have to send them warning signs. God's desire was to be in a covenant relationship of love with his chosen people. Love is the dominant motive in all good families. In the family of God, love should be supreme.

The revelation given to Jeremiah that God wanted his people to call him 'Father' is particularly poignant since the prophet was continually having to bring stern messages threatening judgment. Jeremiah perceived the fatherly heart of God and the suffering he experienced when his people turned away from him and rejected him. Jeremiah himself knew the pain of rejection by his own family and so he appreciated something of God's pain through the unfaithfulness of his people.

Jesus was well aware of the prophecies of Jeremiah and he must have known this revelation of the Fatherhood of

God. His own teaching built upon this, showing that God's concern was not only for Israel but 'God so loved the world that he sent his only Son' to offer eternal life to all who would receive him (John 3: 16).

Our reading today shows that God not only wants to give us good things, but that he longs for us to know him as 'Father', so that he can surround us with our Father's love. This is freely available to us through Jesus, our Lord.

Prayer
Come, Lord Jesus, show us the Father. Help me to understand more of the Father's love and draw me closer to him this very day.

Today with Jeremiah

UNPLOUGHED GROUND

Jeremiah 4: 3-4a
This is what the Lord says to the men of Judah and to Jerusalem: 'Break up your unploughed ground and do not sow among thorns. Circumcise yourselves to the Lord, circumcise your hearts, you men of Judah and people of Jerusalem.'

Comment

The tiny nation of Judah was threatened with extinction as the international scene darkened and the Babylonian army cruelly conquered one small state after another, drawing ever closer to Jerusalem. Most of Judah's neighbours had already succumbed to the enemy and Jeremiah knew that the nation's only hope of survival was through divine intervention.

As God had destroyed the Assyrian army of Sennacherib a century earlier, when Jerusalem was attacked during the reign of Hezekiah and the ministry of Isaiah, so he could do once again. But divine protection was only guaranteed so long as there was faithfulness to God and righteousness in the land.

Jeremiah knew there was much fear among the people but very little trust in God. His stern warnings largely fell upon deaf ears. The political rulers were more interested in trusting pacts and treaties with other nations, strengthening the walls around Jerusalem, and increasing the army. Jeremiah knew this was useless and that, unless there was repentance and turning to God, Jerusalem would fall.

In today's reading, the word of God to the nation is to break up the unploughed ground. This meant softening the hearts of the people to be able to hear the word of the Lord.

The call to spiritual circumcision was a call to be consecrated to the Lord. Circumcision was a sign of 'belongingness' to the Lord through the covenant, but God was looking for more than a mere physical sign. He was wanting to see commitment, loyalty, obedience and trust in the hearts of his people.

God does not want a mere outward sign of our devotion. He is looking for real devotion in the hearts of his people today. There is so much hard ground, or unconsecrated paths, in all our lives. We are part of a self-centred generation and we probably do not even realise how much we have taken into our lives from the values of the world which do not accord with the values of the kingdom.

We need to hear this word. The Lord is saying, 'Break up the hard ground' so that the whole of your life can bear fruit and not just a tiny part of it.

Prayer
Father, today I want to respond to your word. Please help me to identify the unploughed ground in my life and to soften my heart to you.

THE PROPHET'S ANGUISH

Jeremiah 4: 18-20a
'Your own conduct and actions have brought this upon you. This is your punishment. How bitter it is! How it pierces to the heart!' Oh, my anguish, my anguish! I writhe in pain. Oh, the agony of my heart! My heart pounds within me, I cannot keep silent. For I have heard the sound of the trumpet; I have heard the battle cry. Disaster follows disaster; the whole land lies in ruins.

Comment

Jeremiah is foreseeing a time of terrible destruction from enemy invasion. He was praying about the international situation and interceding for his own beloved country. During this time of prayer the Lord revealed to him what would happen unless there was a return to God which would allow him to protect the nation.

When the prophet was in the 'council of the Lord' he saw, in vivid detail, the destruction of the land and he heard the terrible battle cry of the cruel enemy. This caused Jeremiah immense pain. He was a great patriot, as indeed were all the prophets. Patriotism is very different from nationalism. Nationalism is a *blind support* of one's own country, whether it be right or wrong.

Patriotism is a *love* of one's country. Patriotism does not blind you to your country's faults. Your love of the country makes you long for things to be set right. Jeremiah loved his country and felt the deep pain of suffering because of the sinfulness of the nation. It was as though it were happening to his own body. His anguish was such that he found himself writhing in pain.

The message Jeremiah was instructed to take to the

people was highly unpopular. Nobody wanted to listen to his warnings of coming destruction. The rulers were confident that their policies would be successful in defeating the Babylonians. Moreover, the religious authorities, the Temple priests and official prophets, all declared that God would protect Jerusalem because it was the holy city. They thought there was nothing to worry about. They believed they were quite secure.

Despite the unpopular message that brought increasing hostility to him, Jeremiah simply could not keep quiet. He had heard the sound of the trumpet and the battle cry and he could not remain silent, whatever the personal cost.

There is probably no sharper pain than to be able to see those you love heading for disaster and, although you warn them, having your words thrown back at you. Your counsel is rejected and you know that what you foresee is becoming inevitable. If we can feel such pain when someone we love gets their life into a mess and our help is spurned, how much more does God suffer when we wilfully reject him.

Prayer
Lord, make me willing to bear the pain and anguish of carrying your word, even when those around are unwilling to hear, or to heed.

HONESTY AND TRUTH

Jeremiah 5: 1-2
'Go up and down the streets of Jerusalem, look around and consider, search through her squares. If you can find but one person who deals honestly and seeks the truth, I will forgive this city. Although they say, "As surely as the Lord lives", still they are swearing falsely.'

Comment

This is an amazing statement and is reminiscent of Abraham's conversation with God concerning Sodom (Genesis 18: 23-33). In that discussion God first said that he would spare Sodom if fifty righteous people could be found in the city. Following Abraham's pleading, this was reduced to ten. But ten righteous persons could not be found and Sodom was destroyed.

In our reading today God is far more lenient with Jerusalem than he was with Sodom. He promised to forgive the city if just one person could be found who dealt honestly and sought the truth. This was the measure of God's love for Jerusalem and for his own covenant people.

This was also the measure of the moral degradation and corruption in the nation. The people were not being taught the Torah. Moses was neglected, the commandments were ignored. The consequence was a regime of moral anarchy – everyone did as they liked.

A major part of the trouble in the nation was weak leadership and corruption surrounding the last three kings of Judah – Jehoiakim, Jehoiachin and Zedekiah (although Jehoiachin hardly had time to show his worth as he only reigned three months before being sent as a captive to Babylon and the puppet king Zedekiah was put on the throne). These were turbulent days and morality suffered. People probably thought that they might as well enjoy themselves as their days were numbered.

For Jeremiah, the sensitive prophet, the immorality all around him was deeply distressing. He knew that a holy God would not defend an unholy people. But he was not simply the bearer of bad news, of inevitable destruction. He also knew that the city and the people could be saved if only they would listen and turn to the Lord. His was a message of salvation but it was never heeded.

Jeremiah set off on his mission eager to find one righteous person and so to save the city. In tomorrow's reading we will see how he got on. In the meantime, we need to note that God is a God of mercy, but he is also a God of righteousness and he looks for righteousness among his people.

Prayer
Father, make me aware of any areas of unrighteousness in my life and show me how to deal with them.

Today with Jeremiah

KNOWING THE WAY OF THE LORD

Jeremiah 5: 3-5
O Lord, do not your eyes look for truth? You struck them, but they felt no pain; you crushed them but they refused correction. They made their faces harder than stone and refused to repent. I thought, 'These are only the poor; they are foolish, for they do not know the way of the Lord, the requirements of their God. So I will go to the leaders and speak to them; surely they know the way of the Lord, the requirement of their God.' But with one accord they too had broken off the yoke and torn off the bonds.

Comment

Jeremiah's mission to search the streets of Jerusalem to find an honest person soon ran into problems. His troubles began in the markets and the back streets among the ordinary working people. He evidently asked them questions about various national and natural events such as the failure of the spring rains.

Clearly no-one Jeremiah spoke to had any idea that God may have been saying something to them through the things that had been happening. In fact, when Jeremiah made such a suggestion 'they made their faces harder than stone and refused to repent'. The people certainly did not want to admit that God had any relevance to their lives.

Jeremiah thought, 'These are only the poor; they are foolish, for they do not know the way of the Lord'. The people clearly had never even thought that God could convey a message through the weather and through some other event. What was even worse was the fact that they were ignorant of 'the requirements of their God'. Clearly they had never been taught the terms of Israel's covenant with God.

Jeremiah's search then took him to the leaders of the nation. They were educated and must have known the requirements of the Lord – or so they thought! But the result was the same. They too 'had broken off the yoke' severing themselves from the Lord their God. The minds and hearts of both the leaders and the people were closed to God.

When a nation, both the people and their leaders, break off their links with God, the consequences are severe. The moral and the spiritual life of the nation suffers as it did in Judah in the time of Jeremiah's ministry. The prophet was unable to find people who were dealing honestly with their neighbours or in business.

In our lifetime we have a greater advantage than the people in Jeremiah's day. We are able to know the way of the Lord and his requirements through the Bible and through the centuries of our Judeo/Christian heritage. The leaders of Judah had only the teaching of Moses whereas we have the whole word of God including the teaching of Jesus, our Lord and Messiah. There is surely no excuse for the church of our generation. We really should be able to know the way of the Lord.

Prayer
Thank you, Father, that you have revealed your nature and your requirements through your word. Lord, help me to study your word with greater understanding.

IMMORALITY

Jeremiah 5: 7-9a
'Why should I forgive you? Your children have forsaken me and sworn by gods that are not gods. I supplied all their needs, yet they committed adultery and thronged to the houses of prostitutes. They are well-fed, lusty stallions, each neighing for another man's wife. Should I not punish them for this?' declares the Lord.

Comment

This is a highly descriptive passage about the moral life of the nation in Jeremiah's lifetime. His ministry encompassed the last forty years in the history of Judah before the Babylonian exile. The holocaust of 586 BC, which witnessed the slaughter of vast numbers of men, women and children in Judah and the destruction of the great city of Jerusalem with its Temple, palace and great houses, was a direct result of the moral and spiritual state of the nation.

It is a sad but true fact that Jeremiah was totally right in his assessment of the situation. If ever there was a true prophet to the nation it was Jeremiah. He knew the threat from Babylon; he had his finger on the pulse of the nation; he also rightly perceived that the ultimate disaster did not have to happen.

If Jeremiah's warnings had been heeded and the people had been prepared to put their trust in the Lord, and not to attempt to fight the Babylonians or to enter into pacts with Egypt and other nations, Jerusalem would not have been destroyed. In due time Babylon would have been overthrown, as it was by Cyrus some fifty years later, but Jerusalem would have been spared and Judah would have retained her identity and her independence.

The spiritual apostasy of Israel and Judah in turning away from God led first to a moral collapse and then to a physical catastrophe. The neglect of moral principles soon led to the breakdown of marriage and family with the consequent failure to bring up children knowing right from wrong. All this soon led to major problems in the downward spiral towards national disaster.

It all sounds very familiar to us in the modern western world. The great spiritual heritage of our Judeo/Christian biblical faith has been slowly discarded. Up until 1960 three-quarters of all the children in Britain went to Sunday school, but in the next twenty years most Sunday schools closed and day schools abandoned morning worship and Bible teaching. A regular diet of adultery and violence began to be fed to the nation through the media. The result was predictable.

Jeremiah's description of Jerusalem could well fit many nations today. What will be the result? Is our generation any more prepared to listen to the prophetic warnings? Are we?

Prayer
Father, forgive us that we have neglected adequately to instruct children in your ways. Help me rightly to use the opportunities that you set before me to teach and share your word.

Today with Jeremiah

THE FEAR OF THE LORD

Jeremiah 5: 21-22a and 24-25
'Hear this, you foolish and senseless people, who have eyes but do not see, who have ears but do not hear: Should you not fear me?' declares the Lord. 'Should you not tremble in my presence?' ... They do not say to themselves, "Let us fear the Lord our God, who gives autumn and spring rains in season, who assures us of the regular weeks of harvest". Your wrongdoings have kept these away; your sins have deprived you of good.'

Comment

Jeremiah was acutely aware of the sins of the nation. He also firmly believed in the sovereignty of God and in his direct control over natural forces. Clearly there had been problems with the harvest due to a lack of rain. Both the spring and autumn rains had not fallen in their usual profusion to water the land and give abundant growth to the seed.

Israel has always been highly dependent upon rain both for drinking-water and for a good harvest. Jeremiah stood in a long line of prophets who always looked to the Lord for an explanation of what was happening in nature. The prophets believed that it was God's desire and intention to give plenty of good food and water for his people, so when the supply was interrupted there had to be a reason. It was the prophet's task to discover this and to inform the people.

Sadly, in Jeremiah's day the nation had become highly secularised. The two major reasons for this were the influence of Canaanite religion in the countryside and the growth of cities with their urban culture and commercial, materialistic lifestyles. All this had brought about a gradual displacing of God from the centre of the nation. He became redundant in the daily lives of most people. They hardly gave a thought to God, or to the traditions of their fathers, or to the terms of the covenant. There was no fear of the Lord.

In his times of intercession, Jeremiah heard the Lord speak of this: '"Should you not fear me?" declares the Lord. "Should you not tremble in my presence?"' There was plenty of fear of man – especially of the Babylonians – but no fear of the Lord!

God's power is infinitely greater than man's. Moreover, he is a loving and merciful Father who delights to bless his children. We should show respect for God and approach him with a sense of 'awe'. It is so easy for believers to lose all sense of the 'awe' of the Lord in a highly secular environment – even in our worship!

Worship that is acceptable to God has to be 'with reverence and awe, for our God is a consuming fire' (Hebrews 12: 28). This is the teaching of the Apostles of the New Covenant as well as the prophets of the Old Covenant.

Prayer
Give me, Lord, a heart attitude of 'reverence and awe' in my relationship with you, both in worship and in my daily life.

THE PEOPLE LOVE IT!

Jeremiah 5: 27b-28 and 30-31
'They have become rich and powerful and have grown fat and sleek. Their evil deeds have no limit; they do not plead the case of the fatherless to win it, they do not defend the rights of the poor... A horrible and shocking thing has happened in the land: The prophets prophesy lies, the priests rule by their own authority and my people love it this way. But what will you do in the end?'

Comment

The more Jeremiah travelled around the country, the more anxious he became at what he saw and heard. He was acutely aware of the threat of invasion from Babylon. God had explicitly given him forewarning of this. In his prayer times he had seen it so vividly that in his mind it had become a reality. The question he continually faced was, 'How could God defend and protect a nation that refused to listen to him and wilfully broke the covenant he had established with them?'

The gap between rich and poor was scandalous, but it was made worse by the injustice suffered by the powerless at the hands of the powerful. There was shameless exploitation, and if the poor called upon the Law for protection, bribery ensured that the judge ruled in favour of the rich.

To Jeremiah this was an offence against God. It was in direct contravention of the Torah. The combined result of the spiritual and moral state of the nation put the land and the people outside God's protection at the time of the greatest threat in Judah's history.

The most 'horrible and shocking thing', however, was that the real cause of all the trouble in the land lay, not with the king and the politicians, but with the religious authorities. This, to Jeremiah, was unforgivable. The Temple priests and the official prophets failed to teach the truth, either to the leaders or to the people. They were, therefore, ultimately responsible for the state of the nation. They would be accountable before God for the fate that would inevitably befall the nation unless there was a radical change of direction.

Yet how could there be a change of direction so long as the priests and prophets gave, what the people believed was, divine approval to the present state of affairs? The prophets, who were supposed to declare the word of God, were telling lies. They were saying that God was quite happy with the nation, that all was well – no wonder they were popular! The priests had made up their own rules and did not bother with those laid down by God and given to Moses. But worst of all – the people loved it that way!

It may be something in our sinful human nature that prefers the rules of men to the way of the Lord. We face the same dilemma today, whether to follow our own way or to seek the way of the Lord. God's question demands an answer from us today just as it did in Jeremiah's day – 'What will you do in the end?'

Prayer
Lord, grant that all I do this day will be pleasing in your sight. I know that, at the end of my days on earth, you will graciously receive me to yourself.

Today with Jeremiah

PEACE! PEACE!

Jeremiah 6: 13-14
'From the least to the greatest, all are greedy for gain; prophets and priests alike, all practise deceit. They dress the wound of my people as though it were not serious. "Peace, peace", they say, when there is no peace.'

Comment

This is one of the most famous of Jeremiah's prophecies. 'Peace, peace! - when there is no peace' is a saying familiar to millions who have no idea where it originated. They probably know even less about the prophet's life and work.

Jeremiah was appalled that the official religious leaders were unaware of the seriousness of the threat to the very existence of the nation. Worse still, they were actively encouraging the belief that Judah was in no danger because God would never allow anything bad to happen to Jerusalem. They thought the city was inviolable due to the presence of the Temple and its connection with the name and honour of God.

This is the deceit which Jeremiah accused the priests and prophets of practising. They were, in fact, deceiving the people and spreading a false complacency. This was highly dangerous because it covered over the serious moral and spiritual condition of the nation. The false prophets did immense harm because God was calling for repentance whilst they were saying that he was promising a time of blessing with peace and prosperity.

Jeremiah was, at times, nearly frantic with anxiety because he perceived the inevitable result of this false teaching. He used the powerful illustration of a serious wound that is festering yet is simply covered over with a bandage. This is the wrong treatment, as the poison needs to be let out first before healing can begin.

In the same way, repentance and turning away from sin were necessary before God would heal the nation. It was essential that the contamination of sin and idolatry be cleansed from the nation's spiritual bloodstream before God's covering of protection over it could be effective.

The modern equivalent would be the false prophecies which appeared in the western nations during the second half of the twentieth century. These false prophecies, promising imminent revival and exciting times of power and prosperity for believers, did a great deal of harm. It was said that God was going to give supernatural power to his people to enable them to heal diseases, strike down the enemies of the gospel, take control of the airways and exercise dominion over the nations.

These false prophecies seriously deceived many Christians and were a stumbling-block to the purposes of God. He was not calling for celebrations but for repentance and drawing attention to the serious moral and spiritual state of the nations. As in Jeremiah's day, the people preferred the false prophets with their popular message and scorned those who told the truth.

God has provided us with his word as the plumb-line of truth enabling us to test the rightness of the teaching we hear. In Jeremiah's day the people only had the teaching of Moses, but we have the teaching of Messiah himself and the whole word of God.

Prayer
Lord Jesus, you promised that those who love you will recognise your voice, as the sheep know the voice of their own shepherd. Lord, teach your people to listen to you.

ANCIENT PATHS

Jeremiah 6: 16
This is what the Lord says: 'Stand at the crossroads and look; ask for the ancient paths, ask where the good way is, and walk in it, and you will find rest for your souls. But you said, "We will not walk in it".'

Comment

Jeremiah is probably thinking of the Judean wilderness, or the desert of Paran – favourite locations of the prophets, who sought solitary places to be away from worldly influences and human company. In the quiet solitude of the desert they could more clearly hear the voice of God without human interference.

In the desert there are many paths. Some are broad and inviting, others are narrow. The shepherds know the paths and the pitfalls and dangers. Some paths, even broad ones, lead to the edge of a precipice. Often the safest paths are the narrow ones where the sheep have to go in single file following the shepherd. He leads them to green pastures with good water.

David, the boy shepherd, knew the dangers as well as the delights of the desert. His experience is beautifully expressed in the 23rd Psalm in which he sees the Lord as the Good Shepherd leading his people, providing for them and protecting them.

Jeremiah was familiar with the desert. He himself had probably stood at a cross-roads and asked a shepherd which was the good way. He had probably been directed along an ancient well-trodden path which was safe for the traveller. The Lord, one day, brought this back into his mind and it became a powerful word to him. The ancient paths, which the fathers of the nation had trodden centuries earlier, were the well-tried ways. They were safe for the pilgrim to walk in.

In dangerous times, when the nation was faced with great danger and many people were overturning the traditions of the fathers, it was essential to have trustworthy standards. Jeremiah received this as an urgent call from God to return to standards which he had set long ago and to walk in the way of the Lord.

In our own day, when traditions have been devalued, scorned and discarded, the ancient ways are seen as obsolete. We live in a day when everything is disposable – computers, cars, houses, marriage partners – the latest model is the most desirable!

It is surely time to heed this powerful word from the Lord: 'Ask where the good way is and walk in it.' God is bringing the nations to a cross-roads, to a point of decision.

This is also happening in the lives of many believers. When we come to a cross-roads we should not simply run ahead blindly; we should stand still and ask the Lord, 'Where is the good way?' Then we should walk in it.

Prayer
Lord, show me your way and give me the strength to walk in it.

THE WATCHMAN

Jeremiah 6: 17-19
'I appointed watchmen over you and said, "Listen to the sound of the trumpet!" But you said, "We will not listen". Therefore hear, O nations; observe, O witnesses, what will happen to them. Hear, O earth: I am bringing disaster on this people, the fruit of their schemes, because they have not listened to my words and have rejected my law.'

Comment

It was always God's intention that his people should know his word and understand his ways. He had given the basic teaching to Moses, but it was the task of the prophets to keep the people in touch with God on a day-to-day basis. It was their responsibility to teach the people to understand the Torah and to know what God was saying to them in the changing circumstances of each generation.

The prophets were the watchmen of Israel. They had to learn how to interpret signs. These were occurrences in the nation such as drought, crop disease, locusts, storms; or national events such as leadership changes or international threats. The watchman not only had to observe these things, but he also had to know how to approach God. This was what Jeremiah called getting into the 'counsel of the Lord'. There, the prophet recounted what he had seen, and what he knew to be happening in the nation. His task as watchman of the Lord was to observe, to recount before the Lord, to listen to God's response, and then to report to the nation.

Once the prophet was sure of the Lord's response to any particular situation, he was then able to declare the word of God with power and authority. If he had not stood in the counsel of the Lord he could only offer the opinions of men. This was the position with so many of the official priests and prophets of Israel. The preachers and teachers simply delivered little human homilies. That, of course, can also happen today!

In every city there were watchmen appointed by the city authorities to patrol the walls of the city. Throughout the night, when the city was sleeping, the watchmen were alert, looking for any sign of danger. It was their responsibility to blow the trumpet, to warn the people, and to mobilise the city's defences at the first sign of an approaching enemy. If the watchmen were alert and did their job conscientiously, the city would be saved. But if one watchman fell asleep, or was unable to discern approaching danger, the city might be ransacked by the enemy.

In our reading today, God said that he had appointed watchmen, but the people had refused to listen when the watchmen blew the trumpet of warning. A great disaster would therefore befall them for which they themselves would be responsible. They had brought it upon themselves by their evil schemes and their rejection of the word of God.

It is just as important today to have watchmen in the church who can discern danger and interpret signs. It is the ministry of the watchman that enables the church to be the prophet to the nation; to declare the word of God for our times.

Under the new covenant the Lord wants all his people to be watchmen. This was the wish of Moses (Numbers 11: 29) so that we can bring the word of God to our families, friends and neighbours. It is not so difficult to learn to be a watchman when we know the ways of the Lord.

Prayer
Raise up watchmen, O Lord. Enable them to be the eyes and ears of the church and to bring your word to the nation.

THE TEMPLE SERMON - Part I

Jeremiah 7: 2-4
'Stand at the gate of the Lord's house and there proclaim this message: "Hear the word of the Lord, all you people of Judah who come through these gates to worship the Lord. This is what the Lord Almighty, the God of Israel, says: Reform your ways and your actions and I will let you live in this place. Do not trust in deceptive words and say, 'This is the temple of the Lord, the temple of the Lord, the temple of the Lord!'"'

Comment

This is Jeremiah's famous 'Temple Sermon' (or infamous, if you were a priest in Jerusalem at that time!) He was told by the Lord to go and stand at the gate of the Temple, probably on a particular festival day when many people were entering the Temple courts and coming to worship.

The message Jeremiah proclaimed outlined the six major sins of Jerusalem. The first is dealt with in today's reading and the others we will look at on the following days. The six sins are: **false religion; injustice; oppression; bloodshed; idolatry; immorality**.

Jeremiah presented these as the six sins that God hates. His theme was that, so long as these six sins remained in the city of Jerusalem, God would not protect it.

False religion

Jeremiah was probably not aware of Ezekiel's teaching that judgment began at the household of God, but he clearly held the same view in that he saw the priests and prophets as being primarily responsible before God for the state of the nation. Much to the annoyance of the priests, Jeremiah had already said that God was not interested in the Temple religious ceremonies: 'Your burnt offerings are not acceptable; your sacrifices do not please me' (6: 20). Here, at the beginning of his Temple Sermon, he dismissed the popular view that the Temple was a holy place of such importance that God was bound to defend it.

Jeremiah saw this popular adulation of the Temple as a highly dangerous belief which had led to the widespread complacency he found all around him. He saw this as the cause of the failure to perceive the great danger which was facing the city. Until this was recognised there would be no response to the call for moral reform which had been initiated by King Josiah.

This was the reason why Jeremiah attacked false religion as the first of the sins, before dealing with questions of morality. It was folk-religion that maintained the belief in the inviolability of Jerusalem, but this was encouraged by the priests and the whole institution of religious practice. The priests carried out sacrifices and ritual observances on behalf of the people. This left the people with very little to do, in terms of religious obligation, except pay their Temple dues, their tithes and offerings, and leave it to the priests to ensure that God was on their side.

This attitude is probably more widespread among Christians today than most would care to admit, especially in the orthodox and mainline denominations. Eastern Orthodox and Catholic traditions require little more of their adherents than did the priests of Jerusalem. But being a member of any particular church does not guarantee salvation. The only guarantee is a personal faith in Jesus as Lord and Messiah.

Prayer
Lord, I acknowledge that there is salvation in no other name but Jesus. Help me to trust in your name and in nothing else.

THE TEMPLE SERMON - Part 2

Jeremiah 7: 5-6a
'If you really change your ways and your actions and deal with each other justly, if you do not oppress the alien, the fatherless or the widow...'

Comment

Immediately after his condemnation of false religion and the warning not to trust in deceptive words, Jeremiah's first call for repentance, or change of direction, was to deal with the matter of justice. The reason for this subject order is that false religion separates us from God, whereas acting unjustly separates us from other people. Both are to do with relationships, and right relationships are important to God.

Injustice

God hates injustice. When we deceive one another, or cheat others out of what should rightly be theirs, or deny someone their rights, we create a barrier and our actions lead to a break in fellowship.

It is this break in fellowship that is repugnant to God. The Hebrew concept of justice is different from the western concept. The latter is based upon Roman law where justice is retributive. The Hebrew concept is distributive – that is, it consists in right relationships. The just man in biblical teaching is the man who is in a right relationship both with God and his fellow men. If either is out of accord, he is not standing in an environment of justice.

Oppression

God hates oppression. Injustice and oppression go together. They are usually linked in some way. Injustice can lead to oppression and oppression is certainly unjust.

Oppression is the misuse of power or influence. When we have authority over someone, if we exercise it in such a way as to suppress the gifting of the other person, that is oppression. We don't have to be a political dictator like Hitler, or Stalin, to be an oppressor. We can be tyrants in our own family. Domestic violence and child abuse are both forms of oppression. We can be oppressors in our marriage or our friendships when we misuse our love-relationships to exercise control over others and to suppress their gifts or personality.

Jeremiah speaks of oppressing the alien, the fatherless and the widow. The one thing each of them has in common is 'powerlessness'. The oppressor is really a bully who loves to put others down and thereby to enhance his own status.

Weak and insecure men love to oppress women. It makes them feel superior. Men have done this for centuries, both in secular society and in religion. If God has given gifts of teaching or leadership to a woman, he wants men to encourage and support her. It is sinful to oppress her, for God hates such oppression and injustice, however much we may try to justify it with selected texts from scripture. These can, in any case, always be countered by other selected texts. Of course, women also sometimes oppress men, which is just as bad!

Prayer
Reveal to me, O Lord, those areas of my life where I am an oppressor, or I am acting unjustly. Give me the courage to admit it, and to repent.

THE TEMPLE SERMON - Part 3

Jeremiah 7: 6b-8
'If you... do not shed innocent blood in this place, and if you do not follow other gods to your own harm, then I will let you live in this place, in the land I gave to your forefathers for ever and ever. But look, you are trusting in deceptive words that are worthless.'

Comment

The fourth of the six sins of Jerusalem, dealt with by Jeremiah in his Temple Sermon, was bloodshed. The shedding of innocent blood was always condemned by the prophets. It was the severest form of oppression and injustice. God hates the shedding of the blood of the innocent. It was the first crime in history. God roundly condemned Abel for the murder of his brother Cain, saying, 'Your brother's blood cries out to me from the ground' (Genesis 4: 10).

Shedding innocent blood

Jerusalem was full of violence at the time of Jeremiah's ministry. He saw it as the outcome of injustice and oppression. When people care nothing for justice there is no yardstick by which to measure conduct. Men simply take the law into their own hands as they were doing in Jerusalem in Jeremiah's day. It was a case of everyone for themselves. Self-interest was the dominant force. Cruelty and violence were to be seen everywhere, and murder was rife. All this was the result of the nation turning away from God and discarding the commandments.

The people who heard Jeremiah's message would have known the truth of what he was describing, but most of them knew very little of the teaching of Moses and the traditions of the fathers of Israel. These had been neglected for many years.

It was an age of 'enlightenment' and 'prosperity' when new standards had replaced the ancient ways. How similar to our own! Our advanced technology and scientific achievements convince us that we are the most enlightened generation ever to have inhabited the earth. But in the twentieth century, with its global wars and weapons of mass destruction, the earth has been soaked with the blood of the innocent.

Idolatry

This was the fifth of the six sins of Jerusalem and it was one that was constantly on the lips of Jeremiah. Those who often heard him were probably waiting for some reference to idolatry and may have been surprised that it was not first on the list! But this was not meant to be a hierarchy of sin. All six were sins; and sin is sin! Idolatry was breaking the first and second commandments. It was a grave offence against God.

The message in Jeremiah's sermon is that if there was repentance and turning away from these sins then God would allow his people to live in the land of Judah forever. He would protect them and watch over them for good. But they were ignoring the warnings and trusting in deception. Jeremiah constantly warned about deception, as did Jesus, whose life and teaching was arguably closer to that of Jeremiah than any of the prophets.

We are so easily deceived! We think of idolatry as something that happened in the past among primitive peoples. But we are the greatest idolaters of all time. We worship our cars, our houses, our computers, our hi-fis; we worship the sun, sex and material wealth. We are a generation that adulates violence – it is the most popular form of entertainment in the media. We are surrounded by bloodshed and idolatry. And we don't even realise how we are being deceived into believing that all is well with the world!

Prayer
Lord, open the eyes of your people.

Today with Jeremiah

THE TEMPLE SERMON - Part 4

Jeremiah 7: 9-11
'Will you steal and murder, commit adultery and perjury, burn incense to Baal and follow other gods you have not known, and then come and stand before me in this house, which bears my Name, and say, "We are safe" – safe to do all these detestable things? Has this house, which bears my Name, become a den of robbers to you? But I have been watching! declares the Lord.'

Comment

Immorality

The reading today begins with the sixth sin of Jerusalem, immorality. Jeremiah's illustrations are: stealing, murder, adultery and perjury, plus a further reference to idolatry which, in prophetic language, is 'spiritual adultery'.

The whole nation was steeped in immorality. The teaching of Moses had been neglected for many years. Children were not taught even the basic commandments, so the slide into immorality was inevitable. Marriage and family breakdown added to the instability of the times and ensured that children would grow up in an uncertain moral climate, turning to crime, violence and selfish pursuits.

To Jeremiah, who loved his country and longed to see it prosper, it was tragic that there was so little awareness of the danger facing the nation. How could Jerusalem survive against the all-conquering Babylonian army when her people were so dissipated? There seemed to be almost a death wish among the people – 'Let us eat and drink for tomorrow we die!'

But it does not have to be like that! This was the message

Jeremiah gave with increasing urgency. If the people would only trust in God, Jeremiah knew that he would protect them, for he alone had the power to defeat Babylon.

Jeremiah's message ran totally contrary to popular opinion which was backed up by the official priests and prophets and the Temple religion. He knew that he was risking his life in preaching such a message in the very courtyards of the Temple.

The politicians relied on a treaty with Egypt. The military relied on the great strength of the huge walls surrounding the city of Jerusalem which they were confident could withstand any siege. The priests and prophets trusted in the Temple. 'So long as this house of God is here', they said, 'we are safe'.

Jeremiah probably almost choked when he came to this part of the message which God had given him to declare to the crowds entering the gates of the Temple. 'Safe!' he shouted, 'Safe to do all these detestable things? Has this house, which bears my Name, become a den of robbers to you?' Jesus, who probably knew Jeremiah's Temple Sermon by heart, said almost the same words when he overturned the tables of the money-changers and drove out the cattle and the merchants from the Temple nearly five hundred years later (Luke 19: 46). 'But I have been watching! declares the Lord.' This was the real threat to the nation – God was watching! Unless there was repentance, judgment would undoubtedly follow.

All six sins of Jerusalem are to be seen in our own nation today. Surely the same message of warning must also apply to us.

Prayer
Lord, today we want to pray for our own nation in which all six sins of Jerusalem can be seen. Lord have mercy.

THE TEMPLE SERMON - Part 5

Jeremiah 7: 12-15
'Go now to the place in Shiloh where I first made a dwelling for my Name, and see what I did to it because of the wickedness of my people Israel. While you were doing all these things, declares the Lord, I spoke to you again and again, but you did not listen; I called you, but you did not answer. Therefore, what I did to Shiloh I will now do to the house that bears my Name, the temple you trust in, the place I gave to you and your fathers. I will thrust you from my presence, just as I did all your brothers, the people of Ephraim.'

Comment

This is generally reckoned to be the final part of the Temple Sermon and certainly it rounds off the message with a powerful allusion to what had already happened to the northern kingdom of Israel. Samaria had been over-run by the Assyrians some one hundred years earlier and Shiloh – the high place, which was one of the holiest sites in Israel and certainly one of the oldest known locations of religious importance – had been completely desecrated and destroyed by the enemy.

Shiloh

Shiloh was of special significance for the whole house of Israel as it was here that Joshua first set up the tent of meeting after crossing the Jordan and taking control of the land. All the tribes met there under Joshua's leadership and the final seven tribes to be allocated land drew lots before the Lord to decide which tribe should take each territory. Shiloh was, therefore, regarded by all the tribes as the place where they met with the Lord for their first national conference in the Promised Land.

Shiloh became the foremost holy place in Israel and the resting place of the Ark. It remained there throughout the period of the Judges. Eli, the priest, was based at Shiloh and it was here that the boy Samuel first heard from the Lord and became established as the foremost prophet in the nation. Shiloh was, therefore, very much revered, both for its historical and its spiritual significance, as the place where the Name of God was first established in the land.

Jeremiah's words opened up a sore wound. Instead of saying, 'Remember what the Assyrians did to Shiloh', he spoke in the Name of God saying, 'See what I did to it because of the wickedness of my people Israel'. It was unthinkable that God himself would actually have destroyed Shiloh with all its associations with his Holy Name. Everyone who heard Jeremiah's words would have been deeply shocked – priests, politicians and people alike.

Jeremiah certainly had their attention by now! He pressed home the advantage. 'Therefore, what I did to Shiloh I will now do to the house that bears my Name, the temple you trust in... I will thrust you from my presence.'

It is possible that Jesus had this word in mind as he descended the Mount of Olives during the last week of his life. Luke records, 'As he approached Jerusalem and saw the city, he wept over it' (Luke 19: 41). Jesus foresaw the terrible things that would happen to Jerusalem as clearly as did Jeremiah in his day. When a nation chooses the way of wickedness, the consequences are inevitable. But God grieves.

Prayer
Lord, as we sense your grief over our own nation, raise up prophetic voices among your people that your word may be heard.

Today with Jeremiah

THE TIME LIMIT

Jeremiah 7: 16
'So do not pray for this people nor offer any plea or petition for them; do not plead with me, for I will not listen to you.'

Comment

This is the first of three times that Jeremiah was told by the Lord to stop praying for the nation. It is the most devastating instruction any prophet can receive. From earliest times in the history of Israel the prophets had been the intercessors for the nation.

Moses regularly interceded before the Lord for Israel, especially at times such as when the people had rebelled and God was angry with them. The outstanding example was following the incident of the Golden Calf which the people were worshipping when Moses came down from Mount Sinai. God's anger was so great that he was going to destroy the whole nation, but Moses interceded and at length the Lord relented (Exodus 32).

Similarly, the prophet Samuel regularly interceded for the people. On one occasion, fearing for their lives, the people pleaded with Samuel to pray for them: 'Pray to the Lord your God for your servants that we will not die' (1 Samuel 12: 19).

Jeremiah himself, after the fall of Jerusalem, was asked by the remnant of the people to intercede for them, to seek divine guidance as to whether they should stay in the land or run away to Egypt (Jeremiah 42: 3).

All the prophets were great patriots – they loved the land, they loved the people, and above all they loved God. Their ministry was to bring the word of God to the nation and, in order to do that, they had to be regular intercessors, standing in the throne-room of the Lord to hear his word. They could not exercise that ministry if they did not really care for the people. Indeed, it is a true saying that no man can be a prophet until he has first been a shepherd. The prophet who proclaims a message of judgment without tears in his eyes is not a true prophet of God.

Jeremiah was raised for the priesthood and from his youth would have been taught to serve the people as an intercessor. He had a shepherd's heart, deeply caring for those to whom he was called to bring the word of God.

He must have been devastated to hear God tell him to stop praying for the people. Clearly he did not do so, but continued his ministry, pleading with the people to listen. Twice more God told him to stop interceding (11: 14 and 14: 11) because it was too late.

There comes a time when the consequences of rebellion become inevitable. When a nation is so corrupt and refuses to listen to correction, that nation becomes driven by destructive forces of evil which are unstoppable. There is, therefore, a time limit to God's warnings. This is also true for our individual lives.

Prayer
Lord, raise up intercessors for the nation in every town and city so that the forces of destruction may be held back and your word of salvation may be heard by many.

Today with Jeremiah

THE QUEEN OF HEAVEN

Jeremiah 7: 17-19
'Do you not see what they are doing in the towns of Judah and in the streets of Jerusalem? The children gather wood, the fathers light the fire, and the women knead the dough and make cakes of bread for the Queen of Heaven. They pour out drink offerings to other gods to provoke me to anger. But am I the one they are provoking? declares the Lord. Are they not rather harming themselves, to their own shame?'

Comment

Whole families were involved in idolatry. It wasn't just the rich or the poor; it was all ranks of the nation who engaged in various forms of worship of pagan gods (Jeremiah 19: 13).

The Queen of Heaven was a Babylonian goddess. She was known by various names, such as Astarte, or Artemis. She was the same goddess as was worshipped in Ephesus where Paul's preaching created a riot among the silversmiths who feared the loss of their lucrative trade making her image. For two hours they shouted 'Great is Artemis (or Diana) of the Ephesians!' (Acts 19: 34).

As the Queen of Heaven in Babylon she was considered superior to the other gods and was the major fertility goddess. This was her powerful attraction. Her worship extended right across Europe as well as throughout the Middle East and Asia Minor.

The spring festival and autumn harvest festival were of major importance for the fruitfulness of the land and the assurance of a good harvest. This gave her a great hold on the people, who believed she could provide food to feed them! Her worship usually included a variety of sexual practices that simulated fertility and supposedly encouraged the land to produce abundant crops.

The practice in Jerusalem that Jeremiah described included baking cakes with her image on them. All the family participated, children and fathers tended the fire and the women made the dough. This practice was widespread throughout Europe.

Until Christianity came to Britain, Astarte was the spring festival. It was changed to Easter and the little cakes lost their image of the Queen of Heaven and acquired a cross – hot cross buns. No doubt Jeremiah would have had something to say about that!

The word Jeremiah brought from the Lord was that the people were not simply provoking him – they were harming themselves. They were polluting their spiritual lives and breaking their relationship with God. He was their only hope of salvation, so they were cutting themselves off from life.

Prayer
Father, forgive us for our thoughtless ways through which we provoke you. Keep your servants away from all forms of idolatry.

OBEDIENCE

Jeremiah 7: 22-24
'For when I brought your forefathers out of Egypt and spoke to them, I did not just give them commands about burnt offerings and sacrifices, but I gave them this command: Obey me, and I will be your God and you will be my people. Walk in all the ways I command you, that it may go well with you. But they did not listen or pay attention; instead, they followed the stubborn inclinations of their evil hearts. They went backward and not forward.'

Comment

In today's reading Jeremiah again refers to the official religion of Judah, the Temple worship, which had become institutionalised as a kind of folk religion. He perhaps had in mind the word that God had said to Isaiah: 'These people honour me with their lips, but their hearts are far from me' (Isaiah 29: 13).

The Temple worship largely consisted of formal prayers connected with the sacrificial system with which Jeremiah had become increasingly disillusioned. Having had the formal training of a priest he understood the system and was familiar with the practices of the priests. He also knew the teaching given to Moses and this made him tremble for his people.

The blessings for obedience and the curses for disobedience would no doubt have been known to Jeremiah (Deuteronomy 28). This section of the 'Book of the Law' is generally believed to be the scroll which had been discovered during the repairs to the Temple ordered by King Josiah (2 Chronicles 34: 14f).

Jeremiah was a young man in the first few years of ministry when this momentous event occurred. The king had sent Hilkiah the High Priest to 'enquire of the Lord' what to do about the new discovery. It is interesting to note that he did not go to the young prophet Jeremiah, but to the older woman prophet Huldah. Her pronouncement was thoroughly endorsed by Jeremiah (Chapter 11) who also warned that the curses would fall on the nation for non-compliance with the terms of the covenant.

In our reading today Jeremiah repeats the essence of the covenant, 'I will be your God and you will be my people', but emphasises that the covenant requires obedience. God was not so concerned about burnt offerings and sacrifices as he was with obedience. God's command, right from the time of the Exodus from Egypt, had been, 'walk in all the ways I command you, that it may go well with you'.

God is never as impressed with religious exercises as with obedience! He longs to have his people show their love for him and their trust in him by obeying his teaching and walking in his ways. He knows what is best for us and what leads to happiness, health and well-being. He only desires the best for his children. That is why he pleads with us to obey him.

Prayer
Make me obedient, Lord. Help me to trust you more and more, to know that walking in your path is the best way.

LISTEN!

Jeremiah 7: 25-26
'From the time your forefathers left Egypt until now, day after day, again and again I sent you my servants the prophets. But they did not listen to me or pay attention. They were stiff-necked and did more evil than their forefathers.'

Comment

'Listen!' This was Jeremiah's constant plea. His equally constant complaint was that the people did not listen. In today's reading Jeremiah is not bringing his own complaint, but a direct word from the Lord, that for many generations the people had not listened. Since the time of the Exodus they had always been a stiff-necked people who refused to heed the prophets through whom God had sent his word.

There had been a large number of prophets between Moses and Jeremiah, through whom God had sought to communicate his word and give guidance to his covenant people. In every generation there had been difficulties because 'they did not listen... or pay attention'. Yet in every generation, God did not leave himself without a witness: 'Day after day, again and again I sent... my servants the prophets.'

It is statements like these that give us a little glimpse of the kind of conversations Jeremiah had with God in his times of entering 'the counsel of the Lord'. These little fragments of conversation also give us an invaluable insight into the heart of God. They enable us to see something of his deep desire for a close relationship of love and trust with his children.

God longed for his people to recognise him as their Father and so to treat him with love and respect, listening to his words and following his way. 'How gladly I would have treated you like sons', he had said to Jeremiah (3: 19). The pathos in the accompanying word is clear: 'I thought you would call me "Father".'

The father in any human family expects his children to listen to him. He can *command* them to listen, but he should not need to do so. If children have love and respect for their parents they will *want* to hear the advice of those whom they trust.

This is the hurt in God's heart, which comes through so clearly in today's reading. He is saying that we, his children, do not love and respect him enough to bother to listen to him. When will we learn to listen?

Just stop and think of this – when you pray, do you do all the talking? Isn't it time to sit quietly with an open Bible and listen to the Lord? He will speak, as Jesus himself promised (John 16: 13).

Prayer
Lord, teach me to listen to you. Help me not to do all the talking but to sit quietly as Mary of Bethany sat at your feet.

Today with Jeremiah

NO TRUTH

Jeremiah 7: 27-29
'When you tell them all this, they will not listen to you; when you call to them, they will not answer. Therefore say to them, "This is the nation that has not obeyed the Lord its God or responded to correction. Truth has perished; it has vanished from their lips. Cut off your hair and throw it away; take up a lament on the barren heights, for the Lord has rejected and abandoned this generation that is under his wrath."'

Comment

Today's reading continues the theme begun yesterday. God was saying that the people had never been good at listening to him through the prophets. Jeremiah was instructed to level this charge against them, but was warned that the result would not be encouraging. The people were no more likely to listen to him than they had been to the prophets in former generations.

Jeremiah was, therefore, instructed to say that in refusing to respond to the word of God, the nation had turned its back upon truth. There was now no 'plumb-line', to use Amos' word, by which to judge right from wrong. The whole nation was now dangerously adrift in a sea of ethical anarchy – everyone doing as they saw fit – with no ultimate standard of behaviour to guide them.

The people of Jerusalem were told to cut off their hair as a sign of mourning and to go and lament for what was going to happen to the city. A whole generation was being abandoned by God and would now come under judgment.

This was a similar situation to that which Jesus faced when he wept on the Mount of Olives looking over the same city some 450 years later. Jesus, too, realised that the Father was abandoning his generation who had rejected him and that they would now no longer be protected by him, but be exposed to the full might of their enemies.

Jesus foresaw the Roman siege of Jerusalem and the cruel times that lay ahead when half-a-million people would be slaughtered in Judea and the city of Jerusalem would be razed to the ground. 'They will not leave one stone on another', he said, 'because you did not recognise the time of God's coming to you' (Luke 19: 44).

Jeremiah foresaw a similar fate awaiting the city of Jerusalem and its inhabitants. He believed it would happen in his own lifetime. Sadly he was the only one who perceived the truth. Truth had perished and the people were blinded to the reality of their plight. They were not open to the solution to their troubles, because they did not even recognise that they were in trouble.

There are so many parallels with our own day that we cannot but tremble for the future of the nations where truth has perished! But the first step towards effective reform is the recognition that something is wrong. The voice of the prophets needs to be heard among the nations today, bringing truth into the open. As light dispels darkness, so truth exposes lies and paves the way for reform.

Prayer
Lord, we know that you are the Way and the Truth, as well as the Life. Raise up your people to be proclaimers of your truth.

CHILD SACRIFICE

Jeremiah 7: 30-31
'**The people of Judah have done evil in my eyes, declares the Lord. They have set up their detestable idols in the house that bears my Name and have defiled it. They have built the high places of Topheth in the Valley of Ben Hinnom to burn their sons and daughters in the fire – something I did not command, nor did it enter my mind.'**

Comment

Molech was the detestable god of the Ammonites who had been introduced into Judah by King Solomon when he set up shrines to all the gods of his foreign wives (1 Kings 11: 5). Molech was a particularly evil god to whom children were sacrificed in the fire. This form of religious sacrifice was so abhorrent to God that Moses had been given instructions to exercise the death penalty against any offenders. 'Any Israelite or alien living in Israel who gives any of his children to Molech must be put to death' (Leviticus 20: 2).

Hezekiah cleansed the land of many of these shrines on the high places, but his son, Manasseh, reintroduced a wide range of idolatry including the worship of Molech. In fact, according to 2 Kings 21: 6, 'He sacrificed his own son in the fire'. History records that, 'Manesseh also shed so much innocent blood that he filled Jerusalem from end to end' (2 Kings 21: 16).

Josiah had thoroughly purged all such practices from Judah during his reform. In fact, he deliberately 'desecrated Topheth which was in the Valley of Ben Hinnom' (on the southern outskirts of Jerusalem) 'so no-one could use it to sacrifice his son or daughter in the fire to

Molech' (2 Kings 23: 10).

It was probably Jehoiakim who reintroduced a multitude of pagan practices which his father had banished. There is a record of raiders from Moab and Ammon coming against Judah during his reign (2 Kings 24: 2) and one of the ways of buying off a raider was to instal the worship of their gods as a way of showing respect and acknowledging defeat.

Certainly, by the time Jehoiakim was succeeded by Zedekiah (the last king of Judah) pagan worship was all over the land and Molech was re-established in the Valley of Ben Hinnom. Jeremiah expressed the utter abhorrence of the Lord against this wicked practice of burning young children alive.

Surely this gives us an understanding of God's attitude towards abortion. Every day, thousands of tiny babies are wrenched from their mother's wombs, thrown into black plastic bags and taken from our hospitals and clinics to be burnt in incinerators. No civilisation that has slaughtered its own infants has ever survived. Today, we are filling the land with the blood of the innocent.

Prayer
Lord, forgive us.

THE REQUIREMENTS OF THE LORD

Jeremiah 8: 6-7
'I have listened attentively, but they do not say what is right. No-one repents of his wickedness, saying, "What have I done?" Each pursues his own course like a horse charging into battle. Even the stork in the sky knows her appointed seasons, and the dove, the swift and the thrush observe the time of their migration. But my people do not know the requirements of the Lord.'

Comment

In this reading, which is part of a longer piece of verse, Jeremiah hears the Lord saying that normal human behaviour is to seek ways of reversing unfavourable circumstances. When someone falls down, he gets up. When someone finds that they are going in the wrong direction, they turn back.

This was the metaphor used by Jeremiah. He went on to say that the people of Jerusalem did not do this – instead they continued in the same direction. They tried to convince themselves that it was the right way: 'They cling to deceit' (v 5). Even when it was so obvious that what they were doing was all going wrong, they still refused to admit it. They were 'like a horse charging into battle', blindly rushing straight ahead towards death and destruction without any awareness of the danger.

Yet there was no excuse for ignorance, because God had given them his word. The teaching had been given to Moses and handed down from generation to generation. Part of the requirements of that instruction was that it must be passed on from parents to children within each family. So there was, indeed, no excuse.

To know the requirements of the Lord, which were laid down in the covenant between God and Israel, should have been as natural for the people of Israel as birds knowing the times of their migration. As birds observe the seasons of the year, so should Israel have observed and obeyed the signs which the Lord had sent to them.

It was in order to enable the people to understand the times, that the Lord sent his prophets in each generation. Yet, despite this, God's complaint was true: 'My people do not know the requirements of the Lord.' They had Moses and the prophets – there was no excuse for ignorance.

But what about our generation today? Not only do we have Moses and the prophets; we have the Lord Jesus, the Apostles and the fathers of the church. We have their witness and their teaching. We have the Gospels and the Epistles, indeed the whole word of God. Surely we should know the requirements of the Lord! But do we?

Prayer
Lord, open the minds of your people to know your word. Give to your servants the grace and the authority to proclaim it through the power of your Holy Spirit.

Today with Jeremiah

LYING PENS

Jeremiah 8: 8-9
'How can you say, "We are wise, for we have the law of the Lord", when actually the lying pen of the scribes has handled it falsely? The wise will be put to shame; they will be dismayed and trapped. Since they have rejected the word of the Lord, what kind of wisdom do they have?'

Comment

This passage is in the context of Jeremiah's dispute with the religious authorities whom he charged with misleading the nation. The very existence of the Temple encouraged the belief that Jerusalem was safe from attack, regardless of the behaviour of the people. Not only did the Temple worship and sacrificial system encourage false religion, but the teaching of the priests was also false.

The religious leaders claimed to have the Torah, 'the law of the Lord', but Jeremiah's charge is that they had actually adulterated the word of God which had been handed down to them. 'The lying pen of the scribes has handled it falsely', he said. This undoubtedly provoked the anger of the whole religious establishment. This probably included Jeremiah's own family, the priests from Anathoth, who were no doubt embarrassed by their renegade relative.

It should be remembered that the 'Book of the Law' had been rediscovered early in Jeremiah's ministry, during repairs to the Temple under the direction of King Josiah. Jeremiah was overjoyed when this happened and he was a great supporter of Josiah. According to 2 Chronicles 35: 25 'Jeremiah composed laments for Josiah' following his untimely death in battle. Josiah's reforms, however, did not last; the hearts of the people remained untouched.

A major reason for the failure of the reforms lay in the hands of the religious leaders. Here Jeremiah accuses them of tampering with the Torah in order to suit their own purposes. These men were looked upon as 'the wise men' of the nation. Their task was to give guidance to the leaders and people from the word of God. Since their own hearts were not right before God they were false teachers giving the wisdom of man, not the wisdom of God.

Jeremiah asked, 'Since they have rejected the word of the Lord, what kind of wisdom do they have?' Clearly, the answer was that they had nothing more than the wisdom of man.

Isaiah had poured scorn on the wisdom of man (29: 14); so too did the apostle Paul, hundreds of years later, saying that God had 'made foolish the wisdom of the world' (1 Corinthians 1: 20).

Ultimately, the only standard of wisdom that lasts for all time and is never outdated or irrelevant, is the word of God. But even in our own day, there are many wise men of learning, including those biblical scholars whose hearts are not right with the Lord, who use the wisdom of the world, the wisdom of man, to interpret scripture. Their books fill the shelves of theological libraries but they are the modern equivalent of the 'lying pen of the scribes' – full of deceit. They become a snare to preachers and to believers.

Prayer
Lord, give me your wisdom, so that I may not be deceived by the wisdom of men, but may know the truth.

BALM IN GILEAD

Jeremiah 8: 18-19a and 21-22
O my Comforter in sorrow, my heart is faint within me. Listen to the cry of my people from a land far away: 'Is the Lord not in Zion? Is her King no longer there?' ... Since my people are crushed, I am crushed; I mourn, and horror grips me. Is there no balm in Gilead? Is there no physician there? Why then is there no healing for the wound of my people?'

Comment

Today's reading deals with the age-old problem of undeserved suffering. Jeremiah was thinking of the ten thousand people from Jerusalem who had recently been taken captive to Babylon when the city surrendered to Nebuchadnezzar in 596 BC. He had stripped the royal palace and the Temple of valuable articles and 'only the poorest of the land were left' (2 Kings 24: 14). Jeremiah was probably also thinking of the survivors of Israel, the northern kingdom, who had been deported by Sennacherib one hundred years earlier.

'Listen to the cry of my people from a land far away: "Is the Lord not in Zion?"' Has God got no power? Is he unable to overcome the might of Babylon? These would have been the questions in the minds of the captives in exile. Jeremiah entered into the sense of devastation and bewilderment which he knew they were experiencing: 'Since my people are crushed, I am crushed; I mourn, and horror grips me.'

Jeremiah knew that not all those who had been taken away into slavery were wicked. Most of them were misguided. They had been misled by their leaders. He clearly held the priests and prophets mostly responsible for the tragedy that had befallen the nation. Yet in his times of intercession before the Lord, he knew that there was worse to come. He knew the Babylonians would return and sack the city if there was no repentance and turning to the Lord.

For the moment, however, Jeremiah was saying nothing of the future. He was too aghast at what had happened to King Jehoiachin and so many of his beloved countrymen. 'Is there no balm in Gilead... no healing for the wound of my people?' he asked.

The vicarious suffering of the prophet is evident. There is no hint of retribution, no word of triumph – 'I warned you! I told you that this would happen!' Now that the city had surrendered and paid a humiliating price, Jeremiah grieved, especially for the wives and children and those who were crushed by the enemy.

In times of national trouble the innocent suffer along with the guilty. There is no simple answer to this. Along with Jeremiah, we can only cry out to our 'Comforter in sorrow' who enters into our sorrows with us and who sustains us with his abiding love.

Prayer
Lord, we do not look to Gilead for balm but we look to you. Lord Jesus, who died for us and who loves us with an everlasting love, it is to you we turn, our Comforter in times of trouble.

FOUNTAIN OF TEARS

Jeremiah 9: 1-2
Oh, that my head were a spring of water and my eyes a fountain of tears! I would weep day and night for the slain of my people. Oh, that I had in the desert a lodging place for travellers, so that I might leave my people and go away from them; for they are all adulterers, a crowd of unfaithful people.

Comment

If there is one thing that I have learned from years of studying the biblical prophets and exercising ministry, it is that no true prophet ever declares a word of judgment or rebuke from the Lord without tears in his eyes. If the compassion of the Lord is not mixed in with the warnings of judgment then the messenger is not hearing from the Lord but expressing his or her own views.

The prophets never enjoyed bringing harsh words or strong warnings to the people. Jeremiah had the most difficult ministry of all the prophets. For forty years he preached in Jerusalem and throughout that time he had the terrible responsibility of hearing from the Lord and knowing that the destruction of Jerusalem was inevitable unless there was repentance and trust in God. He also knew that it did not have to happen, because God would have saved Judah if there had been righteousness and turning to him.

This was the pain Jeremiah endured. His life was a roller-coaster of hope and despair. He rejoiced at Josiah's reforms, although he had no confidence that they were reaching the hearts of the people. In fact, even the hearts of the priests and prophets were unreformed, despite Josiah's enthusiasm. Maybe the king's mistake was to force the reformation onto the nation. The account in 2 Chronicles 34 concludes with the telling phrase, 'He made all the people who were present in Israel serve the Lord their God'.

Jeremiah saw Egypt conquer Judah following the death of Josiah; he saw Josiah's son surrender to Babylon; and, finally, he saw Zedekiah's revolt which brought on the siege that ended in the destruction of the city. All this he witnessed in a single lifetime! For a sensitive soul like Jeremiah the emotional swings were agony. But his greatest pain came from the blindness and stubbornness of the people who refused to listen to his warnings and so were closed to the word of God.

In today's reading Jeremiah expresses something of his pain and anguish. It is passages like this which have earned him the reputation of being 'the weeping prophet'. But Jeremiah was no softie. He had enormous courage and endurance. He was simply trying to express his deep sorrow for his own people. His despair was such that he could either sit and weep all day or run off to the desert and get away from them all. In fact, he did neither, but stayed to continue his ministry in Jerusalem.

We are sometimes faced with a similar choice. We can either run away or stay and face a difficult situation. If the Lord tells us to stay we will not be alone and we will share Paul's experience – 'I can do everything through him who gives me strength' (Philippians 4:13).

Prayer
Lord, help me to feel your compassion for your sinful people, of whom I also am one.

DECEPTIVE FRIENDS

Jeremiah 9: 4-6
'Beware of your friends; do not trust your brothers. For every brother is a deceiver, and every friend a slanderer. Friend deceives friend, and no-one speaks the truth. They have taught their tongues to lie; they weary themselves with sinning. You live in the midst of deception; in their deceit they refuse to acknowledge me', declares the Lord.

Comment

In this passage Jeremiah reveals a little of his own personal problems which resulted from his prophetic ministry. His own family were very much against him. Here he records receiving a warning from the Lord not to trust his friends, or even his own brothers. He was warned that his brothers would try to deceive him. In fact, Jeremiah's family were involved in a plot against his life. They were evidently severely embarrassed by the prophecies he was declaring in Jerusalem.

No doubt Jeremiah's relatives, including his brothers, would have come in from Anathoth to carry out their tour of priestly duties in the Temple. It could not have been easy for them to hear what the other prophets were saying about Jeremiah. Some of his pronouncements against the priests and prophets who served in the Temple would have left them feeling most uncomfortable. Here was one of their own family attacking the priesthood and threatening to undermine the people's confidence in the Temple and its ministers.

Jeremiah felt particularly bitter towards his family because they evidently tried to deceive him into falling into a trap. He was probably invited to a family celebration in

Anathoth when the Lord revealed to him that it was a plot. He says he was going 'like a lamb led to the slaughter' (11: 19) because he did not realise they were plotting against him.

This incident increased Jeremiah's sense of isolation and the feeling that everyone's hand was against him. He began to see everyone as a deceiver and he saw himself living 'in the midst of deception'. This was a major part of the price he paid for his faithfulness in declaring the word of God.

This is another of the many similarities between the ministry of Jeremiah and that of Jesus. Jesus' own brothers failed to understand him, and the people from his home town of Nazareth tried to kill him (Luke 4: 29). Jesus said, 'You cannot serve two masters'. His own commitment, like that of Jeremiah, was wholeheartedly to the Father.

There is always a cost to discipleship. We may not be called to the kind of ministry that arouses great hostility, but we will always meet opposition somewhere and the need to be true to the Lord is never easy.

Prayer
Lord, help me to be faithful to you even when there is opposition from friends or family. Help me to ensure that my life is a good and loving witness.

DECEPTION

Jeremiah 9: 7-9
Therefore this is what the Lord Almighty says: 'See, I will refine and test them, for what else can I do because of the sin of my people? Their tongue is a deadly arrow; it speaks with deceit. With his mouth each speaks cordially to his neighbour, but in his heart he sets a trap for him. Should I not punish them for this?' declares the Lord. 'Should I not avenge myself on such a nation as this?'

Comment

Today's reading follows a similar theme of 'deception' to that of yesterday's reading, but the context is quite different. In verses 4-6 Jeremiah was being warned about the treachery of his friends and family. Here the people are deceiving each other and the offence is against God.

This is God's complaint against his people. They are full of duplicity and in this they are sinning against each other and against God. Their treachery consisted in speaking with forked tongues. Outwardly they were all being polite and cordial to their neighbours, but in their hearts they were setting traps for them. In fact their tongues were deadly arrows shooting poison into the community. This deceitfulness was a grave offence against God.

A godly community is one in which the word of each individual can be trusted. Their 'yea' should mean 'yea' and 'nay' mean 'nay'. There is nothing more destructive of community life than duplicity. Truth and trust are the basis of good relationships and it was these qualities which were missing in Judah at the time Jeremiah wrote. The stresses and strains of the times, the problems of international diplomacy, relationships with neighbouring states, were all taking their toll on both leaders and people.

The king was weak and vacillating, surrounded by advisors giving conflicting counsel, which encouraged intrigue. Some advocated a pact with Egypt; others favoured an alliance with small neighbouring states to defy Babylon. The uncertain and wavering leadership created a fertile climate for deceit which spread right through the land affecting every aspect of life in the nation and destroying good community relationships.

Jeremiah alone counselled against any pacts and treaties, advocating instead a policy of quiet trust in God. He longed to see openness and truth in all relationships, especially the relationship with God.

When standards of truth are sacrificed for expediency, deceitful practices soon follow. God hates deceitfulness. Not only is it an offence against our neighbours, but, in the eyes of the Lord, it is sin.

Prayer
Lord, help me to maintain the highest standards of truthfulness and openness in all my relationships. Keep deceitfulness far from me, O Lord. May your truth be my guide and my guard.

STUBBORNNESS

Jeremiah 9: 12-14
What man is wise enough to understand this? Who has been instructed by the Lord and can explain it? Why has the land been ruined and laid waste like a desert that no-one can cross? The Lord said, 'It is because they have forsaken my law, which I set before them; they have not obeyed me or followed my law. Instead, they have followed the stubbornness of their hearts; they have followed the Baals, as their fathers taught them.'

Comment

Much of the land of Judah had been laid waste by an invading army. The date of this prophecy is uncertain because this kind of tragedy happened several times during Jeremiah's lifetime. There was an invasion when he was a young man, probably still a teenager. Later the Egyptians swept across the land and actually took Jerusalem, following Josiah's ill-fated mission that ended in his death at Megiddo. Then the Babylonian armies twice ravished the land in Jeremiah's later years. What terrible times to be a prophet! Jeremiah surely had the most unenviable ministry.

In this passage the prophet is seeking the reason for the present catastrophe. 'Who is wise enough to understand it?' he asks. The explanation is really quite simple! The nation has turned away from the word of God, the law, his Torah (literally 'teaching').

It was God's desire that the Torah should guide the leaders of the nation to set standards of truth and righteousness. These standards were not meant to be oppressive but to promote the health and well-being of the people, to enable them to enjoy peace and prosperity.

Israel's problem had always been infidelity. They had always been attracted to the gods of other nations with their exciting festivals and sexual practices. The Baals of the Canaanites had lured them ever since the early days of the settlement in the land. What was happening now in Jeremiah's day was nothing new. They had always been an unfaithful people, turning away from God and ignoring the warnings of the prophets sent to them by the Lord.

To Jeremiah it seemed amazing that the people never learned from the past. There had been tragic results from Israel's defection, time after time, over hundreds of years. How true is the saying that the only thing we ever learn from history is that we never learn anything from history!

In today's reading the Lord speaks to Jeremiah about the stubbornness of the hearts of the people. Stubbornness is part of our unredeemed human nature. It is something that only the Holy Spirit is able to deal with effectively. When we allow God into our lives he softens our hearts. He takes away that stubborn streak which draws us back to the old sinful attractions, time after time.

When we open our hearts to the Holy Spirit he is able to put a guard around us and to warn us of danger, even when it comes in the most attractive guise (as it usually does!). But we have to be prepared to listen to his warnings and not to drop back into stubbornness.

Prayer
Lord, break down the stubbornness of my heart. Soften my heart so that my discipleship is not wrecked by sinful desires.

KNOWING GOD

Jeremiah 9: 23-24
This is what the Lord says: 'Let not the wise man boast of his wisdom or the strong man boast of his strength or the rich man boast of his riches, but let him who boasts boast about this: that he understands and knows me, that I am the Lord, who exercises kindness, justice and righteousness on earth, for in these I delight', declares the Lord.

Comment

The whole of Chapter 9 is a collection of individual prophecies unrelated to each other and given at different times. The other prophecies in this collection are on the theme of the disaster that has overtaken the nation, the reason why it has happened, and the need to lament. This prophecy is quite different. It is a lovely word from the Lord that goes to the heart of our relationship with him.

This prophecy contrasts human and divine attributes. Human beings value wisdom, strength and material wealth. The Lord reminds us that these are not the things about which we should boast. God's own attributes are kindness, justice and righteousness. These are the things in which he delights and which he longs to see in his people.

This prophecy is a call for a re-evaluation of our lives. God acknowledges that there are wise men; there are strong men; there are rich men. But these are not things about which we should boast. The only thing about which we should boast is that we know God. To know God and to enjoy him forever is the highest achievement of men and women.

The Lord wants his people to understand and to know him. Understanding means knowing the word of God and thereby understanding his purposes. It also means knowing something of his nature.

In this statement given to Jeremiah God says, 'I am the Lord, who exercises kindness, justice and righteousness'. These three attributes are part of the nature of God and are therefore fundamental to any understanding of him.

It is surely a great encouragement to every believer to know that God our Father really wants us to know him and to understand his ways. Jesus taught his disciples that he takes into his confidence all those who love him. He says, 'I have called you friends, for everything I have learned from the Father I have made known to you' (John 15: 15). He did not want his disciples to be like hired servants who knew nothing of their master's business and had no understanding of his plans and purposes.

The Lord wants each one of his people to be in a personal relationship of love and trust with him. This enables us to understand and to know him. It enables us to know what he is doing and to understand how he is working out his purposes in our own lives as well as in the world.

Prayer
Thank you, Father, for loving me and for making it possible for me to know you and to understand your ways.

DO NOT FEAR

Jeremiah 10: 2-3a and 5b
This is what the Lord says: 'Do not learn the ways of the nations or be terrified by signs in the sky, though the nations are terrified by them. For the customs of the peoples are worthless... their idols cannot speak; they must be carried because they cannot walk. Do not fear them; they can do no harm nor can they do any good.'

Comment

It seems strange that all the prophets should have had to warn Israel time after time not to 'learn the ways of the nations'. The covenant between God and Israel was clear. He, and no other, would be their God and they would be his people in a unique way. He would use them to work out his purposes in the world, but he could only do this if there was a mutually exclusive relationship between the people and God which meant that Israel was different from all the other nations.

In this message Jeremiah says that God was warning the nation about the worthless customs of the peoples of the Gentile nations surrounding Israel. They were full of quasi religious superstition. If there was any unusual occurrence in the sky or weather disturbance, they were terrified. Their fears came from a lack of knowledge of the one true God, Creator of the Universe. The customs of the people were worthless because they were steeped in idolatry.

The gods of the nations were just wood and metal. They could neither speak nor communicate in any way, so why be afraid of them? Israel, whose God was all-powerful, had no need to fear the pagan gods who had no power over them either to do harm or to do good.

This is a message that many Christians need to hear today. There are many believers who go around in fear instead of standing firm in the liberty through which we have been set free in Jesus, our Liberator and Redeemer. In fact, we dishonour the Lord when we allow fear to have any hold in our lives. The Apostle John reminded believers in his day that 'the one who is in you is greater than the one who is in the world' (1 John 4: 4).

Many Christians today would be scornful of idolatrous practices such as those in Jeremiah's day and would recognise that pagan gods have no power over us. But they, nevertheless, live in fear of witches' covens, or demons, or the devices of the devil.

Many sincere believers today are in bondage to fear. They may know the *word* of God but they do not know the *power* of God. They have not learned how to 'stand fast in the liberty wherewith Christ has made us free' (Galatians 5: 1 AV). This liberty comes, not through our own strength, but through the power of the Holy Spirit. Paul says, 'Where the Spirit of the Lord is, there is freedom' (2 Corinthians 3: 17).

Yes, we are engaged in a 'struggle... against the spiritual forces of evil' (Ephesians 6: 12), and will inevitably receive 'war wounds', especially if we fail to put on the full armour of God. But in terms of our ongoing relationship with the Lord, when we are in Christ, no other spiritual forces can touch us. So do not fear them! They can certainly do no good; but, more importantly for Christians, they can do no harm to those who are in Christ, our Saviour!

Prayer
Thank you, Lord, for your powerful arm of protection around your people. Thank you for your loving reassurance that dispels our fear.

CREATOR OF THE UNIVERSE

Jeremiah 10: 11-12
'Tell them this: "These gods, who did not make the heavens and the earth, will perish from the earth and from under the heavens."' But God made the earth by his power; he founded the world by his wisdom and stretched out the heavens by his understanding.

Comment

The purpose of this message is to remind the people of Israel of the power of God. Jeremiah is instructed to tell the people that the gods of all the other nations will perish because they are nothing more than wood and stone. Material gods are not gods at all. They have no spiritual power.

By contrast, the God of Israel is the creator of the whole universe. He is the one who made the earth and formed the world. He also stretched out the heavens, placing the stars and planets in their orbits.

This message was given in the context of Israel's continuing attraction to the gods of other nations. Idolatry was the nation's besetting sin. In generation after generation the people fell for the same old tricks of deception. It seems that they simply could not perceive the plain fact that there is only one God and that he had favoured them by choosing them as his special people.

Why is it that some sins have such a peculiar hold over us? We should be able to brush them aside once we have committed our lives to God. But the old temptations linger around and cling to us and the enemy never gives up trying to deceive, ensnare and entrap.

This was what happened with Israel. The irony was that

they were the only people who knew the truth. They were the only ones to whom God had revealed himself, his nature, his truth and his purposes; yet time after time they fell for the enticing attractions of the pagan gods.

Israel was chosen by God to be his servant, to be a light to the Gentiles and to reveal his purposes to the world. Sadly their predilection for pagan gods made it impossible for God to use them as he had purposed.

Before we cast stones at Israel and pour scorn upon them, we should examine our own lives. Strip away the thin veneer of modern sophistication and look at the material gods of plastic, metal and concrete which we worship – our houses, cars, computers, videos, hi-fis, etc, etc, etc. They will all perish! There is only one, true, eternal God – the Creator and Sustainer of the Universe. He, only he, is worthy of our worship.

There is a great difference between the values of the world and the values of the kingdom. But can this be seen in the behaviour of those who belong to the kingdom? Is there really a difference between our lifestyles and those of our secular neighbours?

Prayer
Lord, help me to get my values straight and free me from worshipping the gods of this world.

'DIRECT MY STEPS, LORD'

Jeremiah 10: 23-24
I know, O Lord, that a man's life is not his own; it is not for man to direct his steps. Correct me, Lord, but only with justice – not in your anger, lest you reduce me to nothing.

Comment

This is the prophet at prayer. There was no prophet more conscious than Jeremiah of the need to hear from God and to get the message right. He was all too well aware of the danger of getting the message wrong and of misleading the people.

Jeremiah's nightmare was being a false prophet. His highly sensitive spirit was tuned to the Lord, although he did not always find it easy to hear from him. There were many times when he had to delay coming to a conclusion until he was sure that he was hearing from the Lord.

An example was when Hananiah 'prophesied' that within two years God would break the power of Babylon (28: 3). Although this did not witness to Jeremiah, he wisely said, 'Amen, may the Lord do so!' (28: 6). Then he walked away to seek the Lord before giving any fuller response. Once he had heard from the Lord he was able to speak with power and authority.

Jeremiah reveals something of his own humility before the Lord in this fragment of prayer which is today's reading. He acknowledges that our human lives are in God's hands. God is able to overrule and direct our steps. Jeremiah himself does not want to direct his own steps, so he pleads with the Lord to correct him if he is going wrong. He adds a plea for God's mercy and gentleness: '...not in your anger, lest you reduce me to nothing'.

This is the kind of prayer that should come naturally to every believer. None of us finds it easy or automatic to receive clear guidance from the Lord. When we are faced with major decisions that may affect the lives of others as well as ourselves we need to make sure that we are right.

Jeremiah did not find it easy to get clear guidance from God. There were many days when he found it difficult to hear from the Lord. There was one occasion when he had to wait ten days before he got the answer to his urgent intercession (42: 7). God is not in a hurry. Learning to be patient in waiting upon him is all part of our learning to trust him. He will never leave us; he will always answer prayer – even if it is not the answer that we want to hear!

Only God knows the future. Only he knows the outcome of the decisions we have to take. If, after seeking the Lord, it seems right to go ahead, then we should take tentative steps of faith, at the same time asking the Lord to stop us if we are going wrong. It is always good to pray Jeremiah's prayer –

Prayer
'Correct me, Lord, but only with justice – not in your anger, lest you reduce me to nothing.'

THE COVENANT

Jeremiah 11: 1-4a
This is the word that came to Jeremiah from the Lord: 'Listen to the terms of this covenant and tell them to the people of Judah and to those who live in Jerusalem. Tell them that this is what the Lord, the God of Israel, says: "Cursed is the man who does not obey the terms of this covenant – the terms I commanded your forefathers when I brought them out of Egypt, out of the iron-smelting furnace."'

Comment

This passage is very similar to parts of Jeremiah's Temple Sermon in Chapter 7. The emphasis here is upon the covenant. The prophecy is of uncertain date but clearly it refers to the terms of the covenant as set out in Deuteronomy 28. Jeremiah must also have had in mind other parts of Deuteronomy – hence, the phrase referring to Egypt as 'the iron-smelting furnace' comes from Deuteronomy 4: 20.

It is more than likely that this is the forerunner of the Temple Sermon. If that is the case, it would have been one of Jeremiah's earlier pronouncements made during the reign of Josiah when the 'Book of the Law' was freshly discovered during the repairs to the Temple. The discovery generated a great deal of interest and caused the king to tear his clothes in despair on hearing the curses that would come upon the nation for disobeying the covenant and breaking its terms.

King Josiah had sent to the woman prophet, Huldah, to ask what the Lord was saying to the nation. She said, 'This is what the Lord says: "I am going to bring disaster upon this place and its people – all the curses written in the book"' (2 Chronicles 34: 24). Jeremiah prophesied in very similar terms: 'Cursed is the man who does not obey the terms of this covenant.'

Josiah had called a great assembly in Jerusalem after hearing the word of the Lord through the prophet Huldah. The elders of the nation, the priests and Levites, and all the people were commanded to come and hear the Book of the Covenant read. Following this, Josiah renewed the covenant, promising to follow the Lord and to keep his commands with all his heart and soul (2 Chronicles 34: 31).

It is almost certain that Jeremiah would have been present at the great assembly when King Josiah renewed the covenant. It was no doubt on the strength of this renewal that Jeremiah reminded the people of the terrible curses which they would bring upon themselves if they now disobeyed the terms of the covenant.

When we make promises before God, committing our lives to him, we need to remember that there are serious consequences to back-sliding and breaking our promises. It is a serious thing to enter into a covenant with God.

Prayer
Lord, we know that you are faithful to keep your covenant promises. Help me, O Lord, to be faithful to you.

Today with Jeremiah

PAY ATTENTION!

Jeremiah 11: 6-8
The Lord said to me, 'Proclaim all these words in the towns of Judah and in the streets of Jerusalem: "Listen to the terms of this covenant and follow them. From the time I brought your forefathers up out of Egypt until today, I warned them again and again, saying, "Obey me'. But they did not listen or pay attention; instead, they followed the stubbornness of their evil hearts. So I brought on them all the curses of the covenant I had commanded them to follow but that they did not keep."'

Comment

In this passage, Jeremiah was told to take the message about the terms of the covenant to the towns of Judah as well as to the city of Jerusalem. It is most likely that this command from the Lord came shortly after the discovery of the 'Book of the Law' and the renewing of the covenant by Josiah.

The king began an extensive programme of reform which included destroying the high places around Judah which were centres of pagan practices. He also cleaned up the Temple and the streets of Jerusalem from the many shrines dedicated to other gods.

Jeremiah appears not to have had much confidence in the effectiveness of the reform. Some scholars think he actually opposed it, but the evidence for this is not convincing and the historical account of Josiah's death in 2 Chronicles 35: 25 speaks of Jeremiah mourning his loss. It is much more likely that Jeremiah supported the reform but recognised the need for it to go deeper than merely destroying the shrines.

If the reform was to be effective in turning away the wrath of God from the nation, Jeremiah knew that the hearts of the people had to be changed. It was no doubt with this mission as his purpose that he set out to go from town to town preaching a message of warning and calling for repentance. In today's parlance Jeremiah's mission would have been an evangelistic crusade calling for national repentance.

Jeremiah knew that the nation had always been stubborn. They had never listened to the prophets or paid attention to the warnings God had sent to them. Many times the nation had suffered in the past, but this time he foresaw the worst disaster in the nation's history. Hence the urgency of his mission.

It is not sufficient merely to hear from God. We also have to 'pay attention!' That is the demanding part. The easy part is to listen, but paying attention means doing something about it – being obedient to the Lord.

Prayer
Dear Father, when you speak to me, help me not only to listen but also to pay attention!

Today with Jeremiah

CONSPIRACY

Jeremiah 11: 9
Then the Lord said to me, 'There is a conspiracy among the people of Judah and those who live in Jerusalem'.

Comment

The air was full of reform. King Josiah had responded with great fervour to the discovery of the 'Book of the Law' during repairs to the Temple. When he read the penalties for breaking the covenant (Deuteronomy 28: 16f) he was determined to clean up the spiritual life of the nation.

Josiah commanded the people to come to a great assembly, during which he renewed the covenant on behalf of the nation. He then enforced the destruction of the shrines on the high places throughout Judah. But he could not change the hearts of the people. No programme of reform could do that.

Secretly the people crept back to the high places, built their little shrines on the rooftops of their houses and found a variety of ways to continue their idolatrous practices. They thought their ways were hidden from the king (and from God) but they did not reckon with the prophet who regularly entered the throne room of the Lord where things were revealed to him that were hidden from men.

The resumption of pagan worship, even though carried out secretly, was an offence against God. The Lord revealed to Jeremiah that there was a two-part conspiracy. One part was designed to deceive the king (but it was, in fact, against God). The other was against God's prophet, Jeremiah.

Jeremiah's own family and friends in Anathoth, his home town, were plotting against him. This was probably because Jeremiah supported the reform which threatened the livelihood of his priestly family who regularly ministered at the high places. With worship now officially centralised in the Temple, Jeremiah's family would lose their comfortable jobs at the high places and have to perform lowly tasks in Jerusalem.

Jeremiah was distraught. His ministry was rejected by the people who refused to listen to the word of God which he brought, and now his life was in danger. The spiritual life of the nation was utterly corrupt, but still the people thought that God did not know what they were doing.

How foolish! Nothing is hidden from the Lord. We cannot make secret conspiracies that are hidden from him. He knows our inmost thoughts. It is lovely to know this, provided our life is fully committed to the Lord and open to him.

Prayer
Lord, help me to live in such a way that all my days are pleasing in your sight.

Today with Jeremiah

RUNNING OUT OF TIME

Jeremiah 11: 10-11
'They have returned to the sins of their forefathers, who refused to listen to my words. They have followed other gods to serve them. Both the house of Israel and the house of Judah have broken the covenant I made with their forefathers. Therefore this is what the Lord says: "I will bring on them a disaster they cannot escape. Although they cry out to me, I will not listen to them."'

Comment

It is strange how the sins of the people persisted in generation after generation. The history of Israel could almost be summarised in the first part of today's reading. The three main charges against them were: they refused to listen; they served other gods; they broke the covenant.

From the time of Moses onwards the prophets always brought the same message. They all experienced the same frustration – the people refused to listen. The prophets warned about the dangers of following other gods but their warnings fell upon deaf ears. The people did not want to hear.

The attraction of the gods who were worshipped by the pagan nations and the people among whom the Israelites lived was so powerful that they were prepared to risk the consequences of disobedience. Moses had spelled out those consequences very clearly. They were part of the terms of the covenant which God had established with Israel.

In generation after generation, warnings were given that the breaking of the covenant left the nation exposed to danger. Now, in Jeremiah's lifetime, after so many warnings had been ignored, God put the nation on notice that time was running out. A disaster of mega proportions, from which they would not be able to escape, was looming on the horizon.

It may seem strange to us that the people whom God had chosen as the means through whom he would reveal himself to the world, should be so stubborn and unresponsive. But before we pick up the 'first stone' to cast at Israel we should examine ourselves.

We, too, stand in a covenant relationship with God, through Jesus, our Messiah. Many times we break the covenant by our compromise with the values of the world which conflict with the values of the kingdom of God. We, too, do not listen. We are stubborn and say we have no need for repentance. How much longer will we try the patience of the Lord? With each lost opportunity, or warning ignored, time is running out.

Prayer
Father, forgive me for taking advantage of your great patience and infinite mercy. Make me more sensitive to what you are saying to me through your Holy Spirit and through your word.

BEWARE OF COMPROMISE

Jeremiah 11: 13-14
'"You have as many gods as you have towns, O Judah; and the altars you have set up to burn incense to that shameful god Baal are as many as the streets of Jerusalem." Do not pray for this people nor offer any plea or petition for them, because I will not listen when they call to me in the time of their distress.'

Comment

This is the second time Jeremiah was told to stop praying for the nation. It would seem that he had not done so the first time he received such an instruction. One of the major tasks of the prophets was to intercede for the people. Their relationship with God enabled them to hear from him, and they were in a position to go back with pleas from the people. In Jeremiah's case the people were making no pleas. They refused to hear the word of God that he brought, so they did not send him back with any plea or petition.

Every town had its own god and within Jerusalem each street had a shrine to a pagan deity. The people were so steeped in idolatry they were not even aware of whether or not the prophet was interceding for them; nor did they care! Further intercession was pointless. What was needed was not divine action, but human action.

God was willing to forgive and to re-establish the protection which he had given as part of the terms of the covenant. But, first, there had to be repentance and a rejection of the pagan gods. God cannot forgive until we repent. Repentance is the pre-condition. God never withdraws his love or rescinds his promise of forgiveness, but we have to be willing to receive it and our repentance is an indication of our willingness.

We are often amazed at the stubbornness and blindness of Israel. Yet we show the same characteristics! We say, 'How could they be attracted to those pagan gods with their superstitions, fertility rites, sex cults, feasts and festivals, wild music and dancing?' But has anything really changed? Does not the world simply invent new forms of pagan worship? Do we not have our sex cults, feasts and festivals, wild music and all the rest today?

Even if we, ourselves, do not run after these things, we can so easily be influenced and compromised by the world every day. Every time we turn on the television, read the newspaper, digest worldly magazines, listen to the lyrics of sensuous music we are at risk of taking in some of the world's values which can pollute our spiritual life.

We spend precious time and resources on all manner of material things which are of no consequence in the Kingdom of God. Even if we have the best decorated and most beautifully furnished home, the cleanest car and the safest investments – if we do not use our resources to bring others to Jesus, if we do not put God first in our lives we are no better than the idolatrous people of ancient Israel.

Prayer
Lord, open my eyes that I may see my life as you do.

MY BELOVED

Jeremiah 11: 15-16
'What is my beloved doing in my temple as she works out her evil schemes with many? Can consecrated meat avert your punishment? When you engage in your wickedness, then you rejoice.' The Lord called you a thriving olive tree with fruit beautiful in form. But with the roar of a mighty storm he will set it on fire, and its branches will be broken.

Comment

It is truly amazing that in the middle of a passage dealing with the covenant-breaking sin of Israel God can still call his rebellious people 'my beloved'! This surely reveals the tender heart of God. We can never fully comprehend the love of God or understand how deeply we hurt him when we turn away and desert him.

If we human beings can be desperately hurt when someone we love deserts us – walks out of our life to go with someone else – then God experiences that same hurt a million times more intensely. He has given all for us – even sacrificing his one and only Son – but still we forsake him and run after the gods of this world, just as Israel did.

Jeremiah had been told that it was useless interceding for people who were determined not to listen to the word of God. In today's reading God gives two pictures of his covenant people.

In the first picture, the people he loved were in the Temple plotting 'evil schemes' but still believing that they were safe because they were carrying out all the prescribed religious rituals and animal sacrifices.

In the second picture the people saw themselves as 'a thriving olive tree', much valued in Israel for its fruit and for the oil it gave. But God showed Jeremiah that a 'mighty storm' was coming which would send it crashing down and lightning would set it on fire. Even though it looked beautiful and healthy, full of vigour, it would not be able to withstand the force of the storm.

It is easy to condemn the people of Judah, but so often their sins are no different from our own. From village chapel to great cathedral our worship can become shallow and routine. We sing the familiar hymns or choruses, repeat the same prayers, listen to sermons and come away feeling we have done our duty; but in reality our hearts are unmoved.

We are just like those of whom God said, 'These people come near to me with their mouth and honour me with their lips, but their hearts are far from me' (Isaiah 29: 13).

Prayer
Lord, restore unto me the joy of your salvation, the freshness of the love which I once had for you when I first gave my life to you. Guard me against staleness and fill me with a new zeal for your Kingdom.

A GENTLE LAMB

Jeremiah 11: 18-20
Because the Lord revealed their plot to me, I knew it, for at that time he showed me what they were doing. I had been like a gentle lamb led to the slaughter; I did not realise that they had plotted against me, saying, 'Let us destroy the tree and its fruit; let us cut him off from the land of the living, that his name be remembered no more'. But, O Lord Almighty, you who judge righteously and test the heart and mind, let me see your vengeance upon them, for to you I have committed my cause.

Comment

This was the second part of the conspiracy that God revealed to Jeremiah. It was no doubt a great shock to him to be told that his own family and neighbours were plotting to kill him. He had known nothing about it and he felt like 'a lamb led to the slaughter'.

This is yet another similarity between Jeremiah and Jesus. The prophet in Isaiah 53: 7 predicted that the Messiah would be 'led like a lamb to the slaughter and as a sheep before her shearers is silent' so he would not open his mouth.

Jesus knew, by revelation from the Father, that he would have to suffer many things in Jerusalem and that he would actually die there at the hands of his persecutors. He nevertheless committed himself fully to the Father and steadfastly set his face to go to Jerusalem. Jesus wept over the city as he descended the Mount of Olives knowing what was going to happen there after they had rejected the word of God of which he was the embodiment.

Jeremiah knew that his life was in danger in the city of Jerusalem, but he did not run away. He continued to declare the word of God in the streets of the city and even in the Temple where the priests were plotting to take his life. His prayer – 'But, O Lord Almighty, you who judge righteously ... to you I have committed my cause' – reveals the heart of the man. He confessed that he felt like a 'gentle lamb'. There was nothing he could do to protect himself, so he simply committed his cause to the Lord.

The priests from Jeremiah's home town of Anathoth were threatening to kill him if he continued to prophesy in the name of the Lord. They were angry with him, not only for supporting the 'reform' initiated by King Josiah which destroyed the high places where they earned a living, but also because Jeremiah was saying that it was useless defying Babylon – a most unpopular message! The priests supported the false prophets with their popular message of peace, leaving Jeremiah alone and isolated.

It is never easy standing for what is right when others are promoting a false, yet highly popular message. But God is a God of righteousness. When we are under pressure because we have taken a stand for righteousness we can do no more than commit our cause to the Lord and trust in him to defend his servant.

Prayer
Lord help me to be a good and faithful servant, to trust you and to stand firm in love and righteousness.

Today with Jeremiah

WHY DO THE WICKED PROSPER?

Jeremiah 12: 1-2
You are always righteous, O Lord, when I bring a case before you. Yet I would speak with you about your justice: Why does the way of the wicked prosper? Why do all the faithless live at ease? You have planted them, and they have taken root; they grow and bear fruit. You are always on their lips but far from their hearts.

Comment

This is the reverse of the age-old question of undeserved suffering, which is dealt with at length in the book of Job. Where is God's justice in allowing the righteous to suffer? Here Jeremiah asks the opposite question: Where is God's justice in allowing the wicked to prosper?

Surely if God is the God of justice he should ensure that the wicked suffer and the good prosper! But life is rarely that simple! Indeed God's justice does not work out in that way at all. He sometimes even uses suffering to bring blessing to his people. The supreme example is the cross. Through the suffering of Jesus countless millions have been blessed.

Here, Jeremiah was shocked by the revelation that his own family were involved in a plot to kill him. He knew that his only offence was declaring publicly the word that God had given him. Yet he was now a target for assassins. Why didn't God protect him? Where was the justice? He didn't expect justice from men, but he did expect justice from God!

Jeremiah began his intercession by remembering the righteousness of God which he had always experienced. It was because he knew God to be just and righteous that he was bold enough to bring a complaint before him. The prophet knew the Lord sufficiently well to be able to approach him without fear, knowing that God would not leave him in confusion, nor punish him for daring to question his justice.

It was Jeremiah's confidence in the sovereignty of God that caused his question – it was surely God who had allowed these wicked people to prosper. The most outrageous thing was that they were his priests, holding public office as servants of God. The name of the Lord was always on their lips 'but far from their hearts'. Surely God knew their hypocrisy. Why did he not 'drag them off like sheep to be butchered!' (v 3)? This was Jeremiah's solution.

Instead of being grateful to God for revealing the plot against his life so that he could avoid going near Anathoth, Jeremiah gave way to an outburst of anger. He even appeared to blame God for the injustice he was experiencing. Instead of thanking God for his loving protection he came before him with a complaint!

We will have to wait until tomorrow for God's response!

Prayer
O Father, there are so many things in life that just don't make sense. Help me to understand your ways. Increase my love and trust so that I can bring before you the things that puzzle me.

Today with Jeremiah

GOD'S ANSWER

Jeremiah 12: 5
'If you have raced with men on foot and they have worn you out, how can you compete with horses? If you stumble in safe country, how will you manage in the thickets by the Jordan?'

Comment

Jeremiah's suggestion that God should deal summarily with the wicked was no doubt influenced by the threat to his own life that God had revealed to him. His complaint was all the more intense because those who were seeking his life were also linked with the false prophets who were endangering the whole future of the nation.

Jeremiah knew that the message of the prophets whom the Temple priests supported was not only false, but it was hindering the proclamation of the word of God. It was preventing the people hearing the warnings God was giving to the nation. They were, therefore, responsible for exposing the nation to the enemy at a critical period in her history.

There appears to be a note of panic in Jeremiah's outburst during his time of intercession. He cried out to the Lord about the injustice of allowing these wicked men to prosper who were supposed to be servants of God. Then he said, 'Drag them off like sheep to be butchered! Set them apart for the day of slaughter!' (v 3).

God's answer was not what he expected: 'If you have raced with men on foot and they have worn you out, how can you compete with horses?' God left the question of justice unanswered. His concern was with Jeremiah himself. God's response was neither ethical, nor even theological – it was pastoral.

God was saying: 'Look, the only thing that really matters is your relationship with me. You are my servant. All you have to do is to make sure that you are hearing from me and that you obey me. Then you can leave everything else to me.'

When we find ourselves plunged into difficult situations to which there appear to be no simple answers, we have to learn to trust God implicitly. That means leaving to him the things that are his responsibility and not ours. God knew that Jeremiah would go through much more testing times in the near future.

It was the prophet's own maturity that was God's greatest concern. If Jeremiah could not cope with minor problems such as the threats from his own family, how would he cope when things really got bad and the leaders of the nation were against him? In effect, God's answer was, 'Trust me! Trust me!'

That is his word to his servants today. Trust is never easy when we are under great pressure, when we are plunged into really difficult situations to which there seem to be no answers. If we have not learned to trust the Lord in small things, how will we cope when facing a major crisis? That was what he was saying to Jeremiah and he says the same to us today. He has the same loving pastoral care for you, his beloved child.

Prayer
Lord, I do trust you. Help me in my lack of trust!

Today with Jeremiah

THE ONE I LOVE

Jeremiah 12: 7-8
'I will forsake my house, abandon my inheritance; I will give the one I love into the hands of her enemies. My inheritance has become to me like a lion in the forest. She roars at me; therefore I hate her.'

Comment

The context of this pronouncement of impending disaster which God revealed to Jeremiah was God's own deep concern for the people he had chosen to be in a special relationship with himself. The wording of the passage shows considerable emotional depth, revealing the suffering in the heart of God at the waywardness of his people.

It has a very personal emphasis. The phrase 'my inheritance' occurs three times, along with 'my house'. The central phrase is 'the one I love'. It is reminiscent of the word given to Hosea where God said, 'How can I give you up, Ephraim? How can I hand you over Israel?' (Hosea 11: 8). There was a constant tension between love and justice in God's dealings with Israel. Justice demanded punishment, but love demanded mercy.

What was God to do? He had sent warning after warning. He had called a gifted and powerful messenger as his servant. God had been preparing Jeremiah since he was conceived in his mother's womb. Through him God had sent the clearest messages in these days of mounting international crises, but the leaders and the people refused to listen.

They responded by becoming 'like a lion in the forest' who roared back at God. They wilfully defied him. The phrase 'therefore I hate her' needs to be read as meaning 'therefore I reject her' or 'therefore I distance myself from her'. It is the same sense as the statement 'Jacob I loved and Esau I hated', which means 'with Jacob I formed a close relationship, but from Esau I distanced myself'.

Israel, in Jeremiah's time, had become like Esau – unresponsive to God's love and unwilling to enter into a close love-relationship with him. So God had no alternative but to distance himself and to leave the one he loved exposed to the enemy.

How many times do we do the same as Israel? Our wilfulness makes us unresponsive to the Spirit of God; although he still calls us 'the one I love', he is unable to have the close walk with us that he longs to have. He waits patiently and the moment we repent we find ourselves surrounded by his love.

Prayer
Thank you, Father, for your willingness to restore me and for your great love which constantly reaches out to me.

Today with Jeremiah

NO-ONE CARES

Jeremiah 12: 10-11
'Many shepherds will ruin my vineyard and trample down my field; they will turn my pleasant field into a desolate wasteland. It will be made a wasteland, parched and desolate before me; the whole land will be laid waste because there is no-one who cares.'

Comment

In this passage God was revealing to Jeremiah what was going to happen to the land when the Babylonians invaded. It would be as though many shepherds with their flocks trampled across beautifully tended fields and vineyards. They would turn it into a desolate wasteland. In this instant the 'shepherds' stand for the Babylonian leaders and their army generals. The hoards of feet tramping behind them are their armies of foot soldiers who lay waste to the land.

This passage follows yesterday's reading in which the turmoil in God's emotions was vividly portrayed as he wrestled with the decision to withdraw his protection from the one he loved, his own covenant people. Here the scene moves from the people to the land. The decision to hand it over to the enemy had now been taken but not without great pain.

Israel had been given stewardship of the land. It did not belong to Israel. The land belonged to the Lord. It was his, and therefore what happened to it was his decision alone. He had granted the stewardship of the land to his covenant people but they had despised it. Now it would be taken from them and handed to others.

This is reminiscent of Isaiah's vineyard metaphor

(Isaiah 5: 1-7). Jesus also gave a similar message in his parable of the vineyard (Matthew 21: 33-46). The owner entrusted the vineyard to tenants, but when he sent his servants to collect the fruit, they were beaten. Finally, they killed his son, so he handed the vineyard over to others.

The parable virtually signed Jesus' own death warrant as the religious leaders of Israel conspired to kill him. Jesus must have known that the same word almost cost Jeremiah his life.

Despite the most fervent pleading, Jeremiah's message fell upon deaf ears. The moving pathos underlying the metaphors used to describe the scene of destruction is highlighted by the words describing God's pain in abandoning the land to the enemy: 'There is no-one who cares.' In fact this was the cruellest blow of all – God said he would abandon the land because none of his people cared. He said a similar word to Ezekiel, that he found no-one to 'stand before me in the gap on behalf of the land' (Ezekiel 22: 30).

Is God saying the same thing to his church today? Are his people of the new covenant any more faithful than those of the old covenant? Does anyone care what is happening in the land?

Prayer
Raise up, O Lord, men and women who care, who will cry out before you and weep for the land.

GOD'S PURPOSES

Jeremiah 12: 16
'And if they learn well the ways of my people and swear by my name, saying, "As surely as the Lord lives" – even as they once taught my people to swear by Baal – then they will be established among my people.'

Comment

This final passage in Chapter 12 is a piece of prose added onto the poem which so eloquently described God's pain and the pathos of his handing over the land to the enemy. The purpose of this passage is to look beyond the tragedy of the Babylonian invasion, the destruction of the land and slaughter of the people whom God described as 'the one I love'.

In describing the forthcoming enemy invasion and desolation of the land, Jeremiah does not report this as a triumph for Babylon. Quite the reverse! He sees the Babylonian army as a mere instrument in God's hand whom he uses to carry out his purposes. They are the 'sword of the Lord'.

It is God's hand, not that of the Emperor of Babylon, who holds the power to determine the future of the Lord's people and of his own land. Israel must bear the shame of the harvest which they will soon reap, because they themselves have sown the seeds of that harvest. They have brought upon themselves 'the Lord's fierce anger' (v 13).

God's purposes, however, cannot be thwarted – even by human sin. Yes, he would uproot Israel. He would also uproot the wicked neighbouring states referred to in verse 14. These were no doubt, Syria, Moab, Eden and Ammon – who would also be overrun by Babylon.

God also promised in due time to bring them back to their lands. They would then be offered the opportunity of being included in the covenant relationship with God.

This passage clearly reflects God's intention to open the kingdom to the Gentiles. This was also foreseen in the prophecy, 'I will also make you a light for the Gentiles, that you may bring my salvation to the ends of the earth' (Isaiah 49: 6). The foundation of this new kingdom was laid by Messiah Jesus, who gave the great commission to his church to go and make disciples of all nations.

Through the 'crucifixion' of Israel by the Babylonians, God prepared the way for the new covenant when, through the crucifixion of Jesus by the Romans, salvation would be extended to all people.

Prayer
We bless you, Father, that through the apparent tragedies of life you wonderfully work out your good purposes.

Today with Jeremiah

THE LINEN BELT

Jeremiah 13: 1-7

This is what the Lord said to me: 'Go and buy a linen belt and put it round your waist, but do not let it touch water.' So I bought a belt, as the Lord directed, and put it round my waist. Then the word of the Lord came to me a second time: 'Take the belt you bought and are wearing round your waist, and go now to Perath and hide it there in a crevice in the rocks.' So I went and hid it at Perath, as the Lord told me. Many days later the Lord said to me, 'Go now to Perath and get the belt I told you to hide there'. So I went to Perath and dug up the belt and took it from the place where I had hidden it, but now it was ruined and completely useless.

Comment

This is one of Jeremiah's action sermons, or 'enacted parables'. In the first place he was told to go and buy a new linen waistcloth and wear it. Secondly he was told to go and bury it in a crevice in the rocks along the banks of a river. Then finally, sometime later, he was told to go and recover it. When he dug it up he found that the material had rotted and that it was now useless. The interpretation is given in verses 8-11 which follows our reading today. We shall deal with both the parable and its meaning.

The brand new linen belt symbolised Israel. They were the Lord's people whom he had formed into a nation from Abraham, Isaac and Jacob. They had never belonged to anyone else and he had bound them closely to himself as a man binds a linen undergarment next to his skin. They were bound to the Lord in an intimate relationship. But they had refused to listen to his words and instead had run after the world and its pagan gods.

No-one knows where Jeremiah actually went. Perath sounds like the River Euphrates, symbolising Babylon. But many scholars believe he went somewhere much nearer home such as the Wadi Parar near Anathoth, or a similarly named place near Bethlehem.

In this instance, the geographical location is not so crucial. The most important thing was that the symbolism was clear and that the message was conveyed to the nation. Israel would go into exile because of her pride and stubborn refusal to listen to the Lord. She had thus rendered herself useless to God for the fulfilment of his purposes at this particular time.

It is God's desire and intention to call his people into a close relationship with himself. Through the new covenant foreseen by Jeremiah and established by the Lord Jesus, this has been made possible for each individual believer.

But it is also possible for us to break the close relationship with the Lord by disobedience and refusal to listen to him. This enacted parable should serve as a warning to us all to be careful to maintain our close relationship with the Lord and not to compromise with the world.

Prayer

Father, thank you for your great love and patience with your children. Make me sensitive to the dangers of the attractions of the world and the flesh which can so easily lead me astray and damage my relationship with you.

Today with Jeremiah

CAN THE LEOPARD CHANGE ITS SPOTS?

Jeremiah 13: 22-23
And if you ask yourself, 'Why has this happened to me?' – it is because of your many sins that your skirts have been torn off and your body ill-treated. Can the Ethiopian change his skin or the leopard its spots? Neither can you do good who are accustomed to doing evil.

Comment

Can the Ethiopian change his skin or the leopard its spots? The answer, of course, is an emphatic 'No!' The context of this challenge is yet another prophecy from Jeremiah foretelling national disaster and defeat at the hands of the Babylonians. Those whom the leaders of the nation had formerly regarded as trusted allies would soon rule over them.

Judah's leaders had shown no discernment in international affairs. Hezekiah had royally entertained the envoys from Babylon despite Isaiah's protest (Isaiah 39). Josiah had lost his life supporting Assyria against Egypt although he had no need to get involved and even the Egyptian king had advised him to stay out of the battle (2 Chronicles 35: 20–25). Now Jeremiah warned Josiah's son Jehoiachin and the Queen Mother, who were so soon to be taken captive to Babylon.

Jeremiah's vivid description of the coming exile in verses 18-21 precedes the question in our reading today. Those whom the leaders of Judah had sought to cultivate as allies would soon be ruling over them. The disaster that was about to befall the nation was now inevitable, despite the plea of verse 15 to listen to the Lord and to return to him. The reason for the inevitability of judgment was that both leaders and people were so steeped in sin that they could not change.

The whole nation was so practised in lies and deceit that no-one was able to do right. Their ears were deaf to the warnings because their minds were clouded by wickedness. They were no longer able to discern between right and wrong. They were driven by the forces of evil. Like the leopard who could not change his spots, they were unable to change from their habitual ways of sin.

How often do we hear the excuse, 'I couldn't help it!' Jeremiah's answer would be, 'Yes, you are quite right, you couldn't help it! You were powerless to help yourself; but God can help you.'

There are many times when we feel ourselves powerless and driven by circumstances, but these are the very times when we should acknowledge our need of the saving power of the Lord.

Only God is able to break the power of sin, especially those sins that cling to us and seem to come back time after time. We can no more change ourselves than the leopard can lose his spots. But God can change us! He is only waiting for our willingness.

Prayer
Father, we thank you for all you have done for us through the cross of the Lord Jesus. Let the power released into the world from Calvary come into my life in a new way today.

THE DROUGHT

Jeremiah 14: 1-4

This is the word of the Lord to Jeremiah concerning the drought: 'Judah mourns, her cities languish; they wail for the land, and a cry goes up from Jerusalem. The nobles send their servants for water; they go to the cisterns but find no water. They return with their jars unfilled; dismayed and despairing, they cover their heads. The ground is cracked because there is no rain in the land; the farmers are dismayed and cover their heads.

Comment

The Hebrew word for 'drought' in verse one is actually in the plural. Jeremiah was seeking the Lord for his word concerning the series of droughts that had hit Judah. His description in this prophetic poem of the effects of the droughts gives a vivid picture of the terrible suffering endured by every living creature. The absence of water in the land was one commodity over which the people had no control, but which they could not do without.

Everyone was affected by the droughts, rich and poor, young and old, city dwellers and farmers. The whole nation was in mourning; even the wild animals were dying of thirst – 'wild donkeys stand on the barren heights and pant like jackals' (v 5). In the cities the wells had all run dry and in the countryside the streams and river beds were cracked and empty. It was a scene of desolation and death.

In his heart Jeremiah already knew the reason. He did not have to go far to see the evidence of Judah's sins. Nevertheless he loved the nation, he grieved for the land and its people. No doubt he himself was suffering from the prolonged series of droughts. This latest one was probably the worst he had ever experienced. But still the prophet got before God and pleaded for the land and its people. Like all the prophets, he was a faithful intercessor.

Jeremiah had been told to remind people of the terms of the covenant (11: 1), but they had not listened or heeded his words. The terms of the covenant in Deuteronomy 28 were perfectly clear. The consequences of breaking the covenant and turning away from the Lord would be that 'the sky over your head will be bronze, the ground beneath you iron' (Deuteronomy 28: 23).

The teaching Moses had given was, 'If you fully obey the Lord your God and carefully follow all his commands ... blessings will come upon you' (Deuteronomy 28: 1); but, conversely, disobedience would bring terrible curses on the land and all its inhabitants.

It is a serious thing to enter into a covenant with God. It carries awesome responsibilities. Once we acknowledge him as our God, we belong to him; we are his servants, as well as his beloved children.

There are wonderful blessings and benefits from the love and protection the Father gives to his children, but there are also responsibilities. We are his witnesses in the world and if we turn away from him – deny him, reject his word, become unfaithful servants – we bring upon ourselves terrible consequences, both as individuals and collectively as a nation.

Prayer
Father, make us sensitive to what you are saying to us, your people. Help me to know your word for my life and to be faithful all the days of my life.

Today with Jeremiah

THE HOPE OF ISRAEL

Jeremiah 14: 7-9
Although our sins testify against us, O Lord, do something for the sake of your name. For our backsliding is great; we have sinned against you. O hope of Israel, its Saviour in times of distress, why are you like a stranger in the land, like a traveller who stays only a night? Why are you like a man taken by surprise, like a warrior powerless to save? You are among us, O Lord, and we bear your name; do not forsake us!

Comment

There are some beautiful prayers scattered among the prophecies of Jeremiah. This one in today's reading follows the terrible picture of drought which Jeremiah describes so vividly. He is deeply moved by the suffering of the people and the desolation that has fallen upon the whole land.

It is impossible to understand Jeremiah's plea in this prayer without seeing it in the context of his own great love for the land. The land belonged, not to the people, but to the Lord. The people of Israel were the stewards of the land, caring for it as a sacred trust. Because ownership of the land belonged to God anything adverse that happened to it brought him dishonour.

In this prayer, Jeremiah appeals to God to do something for the sake of his own name. The Caananites and Amorites, among whom the people of Israel and Judah lived, believed that Baal, the local god of the land, was a rain god and that if he were not worshipped he would withhold the rain. This increased the tendency towards idolatry among the people of Judah, particularly when they were desperate for water in times of drought. But Jeremiah acknowledges God as the 'hope of Israel, its Saviour in times of distress'.

Jeremiah knew that it was only God who could send the rain. He alone could save Israel. Hence the prophet's fervent plea, 'Do not forsake us!' He acknowledged that the whole nation had sinned and therefore deserved the judgment which had come upon them. The prophet did not appeal to God because of the righteousness of the people, but he appealed for the mercy of God. This was their only hope.

There are times when we get our lives into such a mess that there is no way out. It is at such times that we can do nothing other than throw ourselves completely upon the mercy of God, acknowledging that we have no other hope.

Sometimes it takes difficult or even disastrous circumstances to make us acknowledge the Lord as our only hope. It would be much better to do that when we are not in a desperate situation!

Prayer
Lord, I know that you are my only hope and my only Saviour. Help me not only to remember this in bad times but also in good times, and to honour you in the presence of my family and my friends.

Today with Jeremiah

UNACCEPTABLE RELIGION

Jeremiah 14: 10-12
This is what the Lord says about this people: 'They greatly love to wander; they do not restrain their feet. So the Lord does not accept them; he will now remember their wickedness and punish them for their sins.' Then the Lord said to me, 'Do not pray for the well-being of this people. Although they fast, I will not listen to their cry; though they offer burnt offerings and grain offerings, I will not accept them. Instead, I will destroy them with the sword, famine and plague.'

Comment

Jeremiah's prayer which we read yesterday was a plea for God to 'do something' to save the people who were suffering greatly because of a series of droughts which had devastated the land and brought calamity to all living things – plants, animals and people. Although Jeremiah knew that the drought was a judgment for the sins of the people, he nevertheless cried out to God on behalf of the land and the people. The prophets were indeed the intercessors of Israel. They were the ones to whom the people turned in times of distress.

Jeremiah's fervent prayer was certainly heard by the Lord, but his request was not accepted because the Lord knew that there was no genuine repentance among the people. God had sent warning after warning, but each had been ignored. The people had simply grown more skilled in their wickedness. God had called Israel into a covenant relationship with himself in order to carry out his purposes in the world. But now, because of their unfaithfulness, he could not use them.

God had sent prophets to the people to explain the terms of the covenant and to call for repentance and turning to him, but every appeal had been refused. He was now withdrawing his cover of protection from over the land and leaving it exposed to the forces of destruction – drought, famine, and the sword.

This was the judgment that God had said would come upon the land unless the people turned to him. Now it was too late. Time had run out. Judgment had already begun. The prophet was told to stop praying. No amount of religious ritual would make any difference. The land had to be cleansed, purged from the sins of its occupants. Israel's religion was of no avail. It was unacceptable to the Lord because it did not come from the hearts of the people.

Despite the infinite patience, love and mercy of God, he sometimes has to say that he will work out his purposes another way and with another generation of his people. Every believer should pray that that point is not reached in our own nation or in our individual lives.

Prayer
Extend your mercy, O Lord, to allow the maximum time for people to come to repentance. Show me my responsibility and make me a faithful intercessor.

Today with Jeremiah

FALSE VISION

Jeremiah 14: 13–14
But I said, 'Ah, Sovereign Lord, the prophets keep telling them, "You will not see the sword or suffer famine. Indeed, I will give you lasting peace in this place."' Then the Lord said to me, 'The prophets are prophesying lies in my name. I have not sent them or appointed them or spoken to them. They are prophesying to you false visions, divinations, idolatries and the delusions of their own minds.'

Comment

We all like to be bearers of good news. We know that we will be welcome if we carry a joyful message. It makes us feel good and enhances our prestige to be a popular messenger. It is therefore a real temptation to those who exercise prophetic gifts in the church to say things they know will be well received.

A further temptation comes through sensitivity to people's needs. If you love someone who is sick, you long to see them healed. There is a great temptation to bring a word of comfort from God that extends into becoming a promise of healing. The great danger facing those who are called to exercise prophetic ministries (or those who think they are so called) is to prophesy out of their own imaginations.

In Jeremiah's day there were plenty of people who fancied themselves as prophets. The nation was facing one crisis after another – drought, famine, and the threat of invasion from foreign armies. The whole population was longing for a message of divine comfort and help.

The false prophets had a field day! Their promises of peace and prosperity were highly popular and were eagerly passed around the city of Jerusalem. But they did immense harm because no-one repented of the sins which were precisely the cause of the danger to the nation. If God was going to bless them, why should they consider changing their lifestyle?

A similar thing has happened in recent years. In the early days of the charismatic movement, which began in the second half of the twentieth century, there were many prophecies of imminent revival, none of which were fulfilled. All false prophecy has a harmful effect. These may have actually hindered the purposes of God. While God was calling for repentance and turning to him, the false prophets tickled the ears of the people with promises of power and glory. They grew in popularity and in prosperity. They had their reward! People in many churches enjoyed times of excitement, rousing worship and large 'celebrations', but the word of God did not change the hearts of the people and did not turn them to the Lord.

There are serious consequences of false prophecy, of declaring that God has said something which he did not say. If we say that God has said that an event will take place which does not happen, there is a danger of giving the impression that God is a liar or that he does not keep his promises. That is why false prophecy is actually a serious sin. It is also a serious sin to deceive the people and to stop them from hearing the true word of the Lord. We will be held accountable for what we declare in the name of the Lord.

Prayer
Lord, keep back your servant from uttering falsehoods in your name. Help me to ensure that I only speak the truth.

CARING FOR OTHERS

Jeremiah 14: 19–21
Have you rejected Judah completely? Do you despise Zion? Why have you afflicted us so that we cannot be healed? We hoped for peace but no good has come, for a time of healing but there is only terror. O Lord, we acknowledge our wickedness and the guilt of our fathers; we have indeed sinned against you. For the sake of your name do not despise us; do not dishonour your glorious throne. Remember your covenant with us and do not break it.

Comment

This is another fragment from one of Jeremiah's prayers, which is particularly precious because it shows us a side of Jeremiah's character which we rarely see. So many of his recorded words are calling for repentance or exposing sin and corruption, that we could easily gain the impression that Jeremiah was a harsh, unfeeling man. This, of course, is dispelled by the passages where Jeremiah describes his tears. But some of his tears were undoubtedly shed for himself, as when he bewailed the day he was born (15: 10).

This prayer, which appears to be the continuation of verses 7–9, is unique in the whole book of Jeremiah in that it uses the first person plural form when referring to the sins of the nation. (The only other such reference in is 8: 14.) The significance of this prayer is that, here, the prophet is identifying with the people in his intercession. He is not only interceding on behalf of the people, but actually identifying with their sinfulness.

This is reminiscent of the prayer of Ezra on his return from exile when he found that so many of his countrymen had intermarried and turned away from God. He felt the sins of the people so deeply that he identified with them as though they were his own sins and wept before God (Ezra 9: 15 – 10: 1).

Another outstanding prayer where the prophet felt the sins of the people as though they were his own is found in Daniel 9. Although a righteous man, Daniel was able to pray, 'We have sinned and done wrong. We have been wicked and have rebelled' (Daniel 9: 5).

This is the most powerful form of intercession, when the prophet feels so ashamed of sin in the nation that he feels the whole land and all its inhabitants to be contaminated. He himself is part of a generation that has turned its back upon God. He can do no more than throw himself upon the mercy of God and cry out, 'We acknowledge our wickedness and the guilt of our fathers. We have sinned against you ... Remember your covenant with us.'

The supreme example of identifying with sinners is found in the incarnation wherein the Lord Jesus 'who, being in the very nature of God ... made himself nothing ... humbled himself and became obedient to death – even death on a cross!' (Philippians 2: 6–8). If God so loved the world, should we not be able to humble ourselves before the Lord on behalf of those whom we love; however sinful they are!

Prayer
Lord, increase my humility in coming before you. Show me how to intercede on behalf of others.

Today with Jeremiah

LET MY PEOPLE GO!

Jeremiah 15: 1–3a
Then the Lord said to me: 'Even if Moses and Samuel were to stand before me, my heart would not go out to this people. Send them away from my presence! Let them go! And if they ask you, "Where shall we go?" tell them, "This is what the Lord says: Those destined for death, to death; those for the sword, to the sword; those for starvation, to starvation; those for captivity, to captivity." I will send four kinds of destroyers against them', declares the Lord.

Comment

This is probably the most terrifying prophecy in the whole book of Jeremiah. It certainly does not make pleasant reading, even today, more than 2,500 years later. But if we think of it in its historical context, it has an important message that is of contemporary significance.

Jeremiah had done everything humanly possible to carry out his duty as the mouthpiece of God to his generation. He had delivered the warnings, described the danger, shown how the disaster could be avoided by trust in God, but all his words had been ignored. He had also interceded on behalf of the nation with all the passion and eloquence at his command. Time after time God had responded with further messages of warning.

In yesterday's reading we heard Jeremiah's fervent plea in which the prophet had added power to his prayer by identifying with the people and crying out to God for forgiveness and mercy. Surely the Lord would hear such a powerful plea! It was the most passionate request for God's help in all Jeremiah's recorded words. Yet it received the most devastating and final rejection of any word from God. The three elements of judgment – disease, the sword, and famine – are joined by a fourth, captivity. It is almost a foreshadow of the four horsemen of the apocalypse (Revelation 6).

The message was that judgment was now inevitable. There were no excuses. The popular cry was, 'The fathers have eaten sour grapes and the children's teeth are set on edge' (Ezekiel 18: 2). That excuse was no longer effective. This generation had behaved more wickedly than their fathers (Jeremiah 16: 12).

They could not go on blaming Manasseh – they themselves were just as greedy, deceitful, adulterous and idolatrous. They had had ample chance to repent and change their ways. Now, at last, God was reversing the command he had sent to Pharoah via Moses, 'Let my people go!' (Exodus 6: 6). At that time, the message had been to release the Lord's people *from* slavery. Now, it was to banish them *into* slavery.

Surely we should learn from this for our own generation. How much longer can we go on ignoring the warning signs and testing the patience and mercy of God?

Prayer
Lord have mercy upon us. Bring your people to an understanding of how you regard the sins of this generation. Bring a spirit of repentance upon your people.

Today with Jeremiah

DEALING WITH IMPATIENCE

Jeremiah 15: 10-11
Alas, my mother, that you gave me birth, a man with whom the whole land strives and contends! I have neither lent nor borrowed, yet everyone curses me. The Lord said, 'Surely I will deliver you for a good purpose; surely I will make your enemies plead with you in times of disaster and times of distress.'

Comment

Poor Jeremiah! Everyone's hand was against him. Even his own family were plotting to kill him; 'everyone curses me'. This outburst occurred at one of the really low points in the prophet's life. There were quite a number of those because he had to endure opposition throughout his life.

In the final days of Jerusalem, when the city was under siege, he was imprisoned and even dropped down a well and left to die. He was saved by a friendly official in the court who pleaded with the king on his behalf (Jeremiah 38).

Jeremiah is often known as 'the weeping prophet', a man of doom and gloom. Yet this is quite an unfair characterisation. Certainly he wept for the land and for his people, and certainly he brought graphic warnings of disaster. But he also brought some of the most beautiful messages of hope and renewal, including the promise of the new covenant.

The major reason for Jeremiah's personal problems lay in his own impatience to see the word of God fulfilled. His warnings of dire catastrophe, his calls for repentance, his opposition to idolatry, immorality and religious hypocrisy were deeply unpopular. He was hitting at the pleasures and superstitions of the people and they did not want to change their ways. This made Jeremiah impatient.

As the years passed and the prophesied disaster did not take place, people became scornful and ridiculed him. The false prophets of revival were popular and gained in prestige. Then Jeremiah himself was accused of being a false prophet. This was the most terrible indictment against a true and faithful prophet of the Lord.

Perhaps at this stage Jeremiah really reached the lowest point in his life. He cried out to God to know why he was being given a prophecy that God was not fulfilling. He was so miserable that he even rued the day he was born. God's promise was that he would surely deliver him and that the day of disaster would certainly come. Then his enemies would come pleading for help – begging him to intercede for them.

We all grow weary and discouraged at times – even the great prophets did. But God never ignores our cries to him. He says, 'Now just be patient for a while longer so that I can put everything in place to accomplish my good purposes'. The dark days of depression will give way to days of rejoicing. The light and joy of the Lord will surround you in his own good timing.

Prayer
Lord, help me to be patient and to grow in trust, so that you can work out your purposes for my life and for those around me.

Today with Jeremiah

LONELINESS AND DOUBT

Jeremiah 15: 16-18
When your words came, I ate them; they were my joy and my heart's delight, for I bear your name, O Lord God Almighty. I never sat in the company of revellers, never made merry with them; I sat alone because your hand was on me and you had filled me with indignation. Why is my pain unending and my wound grievous and incurable? Will you be to me like a deceptive brook, like a spring that fails?

Comment

Jeremiah was lonely. He had been forbidden to marry or to have children (16: 2). This was part of the price of his prophetic calling. He would not bring children into a generation that was destined to be destroyed by disease, famine and war (16: 4). Not only was he denied the comfort of marriage, of a home, wife and children; he was also no longer welcome in his own childhood family home. The ministry he was exercising was offensive to his priestly family in Anathoth, from which he was banished.

Today's reading sounds a lot like 'self pity': 'I never sat in the company of revellers, never made merry ... I sat alone.' These words give a compelling picture of the solitary prophet who felt separated from the world, and even from his own family, by the ministry to which he was called. His loyalty to God came first in his life. He had no ambition other than to serve the Lord and faithfully deliver the messages he was given.

His loneliness would have been bearable if he had had the satisfaction of seeing a positive response to his ministry. If he had been readily accepted as a prophet; if the message he proclaimed had been recognised as coming from God; if the people had repented in sackcloth and ashes, and there had been a real turning to God – what joy there would have been in his heart and what satisfaction! He could have endured the lack of a normal home life and human comfort if only he could have seen his ministry being effective.

In the early days of his ministry, Jeremiah found great joy in hearing from the Lord and he willingly accepted the isolation it entailed. It was a cost worth bearing. But as his prophecies of impending disaster went unfulfilled year after year, and the scorn and hostility of the whole nation increased, he began to doubt his prophetic calling. Jeremiah was unsure of the veracity of the message he was giving to the nation which was causing him so much pain. He even went so far as to doubt the integrity of God. Was God really to be trusted, or was he like a 'deceptive brook' or dried-up stream which appeared attractive but from which the weary traveller could not quench his thirst?

Poor Jeremiah. In the depth of his loneliness and misery, he actually began to doubt everything – his calling as a prophet, the ministry he exercised, even God himself. He lost his peace.

It is, perhaps, a comfort to us to know that one of the greatest and most faithful servants of God should have gone through such a time of doubt. None of us is so strong that we can never have any doubts. But God understands our weaknesses. We must wait until tomorrow to see God's response.

Prayer
Lord, I believe. Help me in my unbelief. Strengthen my faith in you, O Lord, that my life may be more effective in your service.

GOD'S RESPONSE – RESTORATION OF THE PROPHET

Jeremiah 15: 19-20
Therefore this is what the Lord says: 'If you repent, I will restore you that you may serve me; if you utter worthy, not worthless, words, you will be my spokesman. Let this people turn to you, but you must not turn to them. I will make you a wall to this people, a fortified wall of bronze; they will fight against you but will not overcome you, for I am with you to rescue and save you', declares the Lord.

Comment

God's response to Jeremiah's doubts was similar to his dealing with the prophet's impatience. He does not offer some soothing words of comfort. There is nothing sentimental in the nature of God. His yea is yea and his nay is nay. That is not a denial of his love, or gentleness, or mercy. Quite the contrary! God's wisdom is so much greater than ours. He sees our *real* needs.

In Jeremiah's case his need was not for smooth talk, or sugary comfort, but for strength to go on with his work. A condition of receiving that divine strength was trust in God. It was a bit of a 'chicken and egg' situation. Which came first: trust in God, or God's strength to trust and to serve him?

The promise of God's strength was linked with two conditions. The first was repentance and the second was separation from the world. Repentance had to come first because, in his doubts, Jeremiah had actually gone so far as to question God's integrity. He asked God if he had been deceiving him by giving him messages of imminent disaster in the nation unless there was repentance.

The people had not repented but no disaster had happened. What was the prophet to think? He had been giving the same message for thirty years. People no longer listened to him. But in Jeremiah's view it was God's integrity, not his own, that was at risk. Of this attitude Jeremiah had to repent.

God was not yet ready to bring judgment upon the nation. He wanted the message of warning and the call to repentance to continue going out. It was a hard task for the prophet, but God was reluctant to bring disaster on the nation which he had called to be his servant and with whom he had made a covenant. Only God knew the terrible suffering that would come upon the people he loved. If Jeremiah could weep for them, God's sorrow was a million times greater. If he could be patient and still hold out the hope that the people would turn, then Jeremiah also should be willing to be patient, despite his personal discomfort. It was expedient that one man should suffer for the people. That was the price of being the servant of God.

But God never gives a task without equipping the servant. He gives the 'enabling' day by day. God's promise was to surround the prophet with a 'fortified wall of bronze' and all the strength he could need. But he himself had to guard against being influenced by the world. The values of the people were not godly and the prophet must not look around in envy of the rich or the wicked who appeared to be enjoying sumptuous lifestyles. Their day of reckoning would come.

There are times when God simply calls us to trust him and to leave the outcome to him. If we remain faithful, despite the hardships, he will supply the strength and protection we need. It does not come in advance, or all in one day. We have to learn to trust God each day. But he will never desert us or leave us alone.

Prayer
Lord, as the manna in the wilderness fell each day, sufficient for that day alone, help me to trust you for strength for today.

GOD'S RESPONSE – RESTORATION OF THE PEOPLE

Jeremiah 16: 14-15
'However, the days are coming', declares the Lord, 'when men will no longer say, "As surely as the Lord lives, who brought the Israelites up out of Egypt", but they will say, "As surely as the Lord lives, who brought the Israelites up out of the land of the north and out of the countries where he had banished them". For I will restore them to the land I gave to their forefathers.'

Comment

This prophecy, coming as it does in the middle of Chapter 16, may appear to be strangely out of place. The entire chapter is about the disasters which are coming upon Judah. Suddenly, in the middle of the dire predictions comes this promise of restoration. It seems quite out of place here and somewhat out of harmony with the context. Yet it is an important part of the message Jeremiah was given and an essential element in God's plans for the nation.

The northern kingdom of Israel had gone into exile about one hundred years before Jeremiah's ministry. Her sister nation in the south, far from learning lessons from that tragedy, had added to the sins of Israel. Judah was even more idolatrous, with shrines to foreign gods on every street corner in Jerusalem and in every town and village in the country. The lifestyle of the nation was one of carefree indifference to the warning signs which were all around.

King Zedekiah had recklessly followed the advice of the pro-Egyptian party in Jerusalem. Instead of continuing quietly to pay tribute to Babylon and to live in peace, he declared total independence from Babylon, relying upon Egypt's protection. There could only be one end to this – the invasion of Judah by the full might of the Chaldean armies with their reputation for ruthless cruelty. Only Jeremiah appeared to recognise the danger and the helplessness of tiny Judah attempting to stand against the merciless might of Babylon.

But it was not God's intention to destroy Judah entirely. He still maintained his covenant with his people even though they had broken its terms. So here in the midst of a description of what would happen when the Babylonian army brought devastation to the land, we have this message of restoration.

It is more than just a ray of hope as Judah's darkest hour approached. It was a promise that God would never forget his people, that although they would go into exile, he would deliver them. In fact the promised deliverance from the 'land of the north' (usually a code phrase for Babylon) would be a miracle of such magnitude that the exodus from Egypt many centuries earlier would pale into insignificance. The deliverance from slavery in Egypt was the greatest event in the history of Israel, so what is here being promised was something beyond human imagination.

God's love for us is unbreakable. Even when our own actions bring tragedy or disaster into our lives, he remains faithful and promises restoration. As soon as we turn to him, he answers; even if we drift far from him, he still looks for a way to restore us and to draw us back into the centre of his will and his blessings.

Prayer
Lord, how can we express our thanksgiving to you for your unbreakable love? Help me to reflect some of your faithfulness and your love in my relationships with others.

Today with Jeremiah

MISPLACED TRUST

Jeremiah 17: 4a and 5-6a
'Through your own fault you will lose the inheritance I gave you...' This is what the Lord says: 'Cursed is the one who trusts in man, who depends on flesh for his strength and whose heart turns away from the Lord. He will be like a bush in the wastelands; he will not see prosperity when it comes.'

Comment

This is a section from what is really a two-part prophecy. The first half, which we are reading today, deals with what happens when we put our trust in human beings – in men and women. The second part, which is tomorrow's reading, deals with what happens when we put our trust in God.

The prophet speaks of 'one who trusts in man'. The background here is the political decision of Judah's rulers to enter into a treaty with Egypt. Jeremiah saw this as entrusting the destiny of the nation to an unreliable foreign power. It was an act of treachery to God. It showed a lack of trust in God, because those who depended upon human strength were those 'whose heart turns away from the Lord'.

The key word here is 'trust'. Israel had no trust in God. They relied on their own wisdom and strength. They put their trust in material things; the strength of their army; or the pact they had made with Egypt, which no doubt carried trade and other advantages.

The consequence of this lack of trust in God was going to be very serious – so serious that the whole heritage of the nation was at risk. God would withdraw his protection and they would be enslaved by their enemies.

Those who rely solely on human strength and resources will not truly prosper. Material things and worldly values lead to impoverished lives. There may be an outward show of success but true prosperity is a state of harmony with God and inner peace. It is not dependent upon material riches.

The biblical concept of prosperity is strikingly illustrated in the account of Joseph who was sold into slavery by his brothers, falsely accused and imprisoned; but while in prison the Lord 'prospered' him (Genesis 39: 23). This turns upside down our western understanding of prosperity!

The Hebrew word sometimes translated 'prosperity' is *shalom*. Many believers have heard this word before and think of it simply as 'peace'. However, its deeper root meaning is, in fact, 'completeness, wholeness, wellbeing'. Biblical prosperity is a state of mind and spirit, not a measure of material wealth. The one who trusts in man (or mammon) and depends upon flesh (the world) cannot know the inner peace which is not dependent upon riches, but comes from God.

Prayer
Lord, protect me from depending upon flesh; fill me with your shalom.

Today with Jeremiah

TRUST IN THE LORD

Jeremiah 17: 7-8
'But blessed is the man who trusts in the Lord, whose confidence is in him. He will be like a tree planted by the water that sends out its roots by the stream. It does not fear when heat comes; its leaves are always green. It has no worries in a year of drought and never fails to bear fruit.'

Comment

This is the second half of the two-part prophecy which we began to read yesterday. It contrasts trust in God with trust in man. The one who trusts in man and depends upon flesh, is cursed; but the one who trusts in God and whose confidence is in him, is blessed.

There is no mid-way compromise in God's values. This is underlined by the terms of the covenant in Deuteronomy 28 where obedience results in blessing and disobedience brings curses. It is probably this pronouncement that Jeremiah has in mind in this prophecy. This part of the 'Book of the Law' is generally believed to be the scroll which was found during repairs to the Temple carried out by King Josiah's orders. Jeremiah was just a young man when this occurred but it made an indelible impression upon him that was to last throughout his ministry.

In today's reading, the contrast between trust in man and trust in the Lord, is expressed in the metaphors attached to each condition. The one who trusts in man was said to be like a 'bush in the wastelands', living in parched, dry and unproductive land. By contrast the one who trusts in the Lord will be like 'a tree planted by the water'. It is continually fed from the stream.

This is a beautiful metaphor that speaks of the whole life of the tree – the roots, the leaves, then the fruit. First the roots were fed by the stream, then came the leaves which were always green and finally there came the fruit. All are fed from the stream which is a symbol of the life-giving Spirit of God. It may be that, while meditating upon this prophecy, Ezekiel gained the revelation of the 'river of life' (Ezekiel 47) which so vividly portrayed the renewal of the land after the devastation of the Babylonian exile.

Here was a tree that never failed to bear fruit and which had no worries in a year of drought. And this is the promise of the Lord to those who trust in him. The life-giving Spirit of God is given in full measure to those who are prepared to put their full confidence in him. Those whose confidence is in the Lord find that he takes away fear and worry, for he is able to do all things, even far beyond our expectations.

Prayer
Thank you father for the precious gift of your Holy Spirit. Increase my trust and confidence in you so that my life is like the tree planted by the stream.

Today with Jeremiah

SEARCH THE HEART

Jeremiah 17: 9-10

The heart is deceitful above all things and beyond cure. Who can understand it? 'I the Lord search the heart and examine the mind, to reward a man according to his conduct, according to what his deeds deserve.'

Comment

The statement that the human heart is 'deceitful above all things' sounds more like a saying from the Hebrew wisdom literature rather than a pronouncement of the prophet Jeremiah. It may be that he was using a well known saying from the Jewish sages and adding the response from the Lord, 'I search the heart and examine the mind'. Jeremiah sees this as an important counter to the despairing sigh, 'Who can understand it?' He was saying very firmly that it is not true that no-one can understand the human heart; certainly, God can!

It was a dangerous belief that no-one could read another's thoughts. It gave ground to the popular notion that God could not see what the people were doing or thinking. They believed that they were able to worship their idols in secret – that their ways were hidden from the Lord. Jeremiah said that God not only sees and hears what each one is doing, but that he is also a God of justice and therefore rewards each one according to his deeds.

The description of the heart as 'beyond cure' (NIV) needs some explanation. The renderings 'desperately wicked' (AV) and 'desperately corrupt' (RSV) also do not do justice to the thought which Jeremiah is trying to convey. The same Hebrew word is used in verse 16. There we read of a day of 'disaster' (RSV), of 'despair' (NIV), a 'woeful' day (AV). Elsewhere, the AV translates it as 'incurable', eg 15: 18 and 30: 12 & 15.

Probably the best translation for the word in today's reading is that of the NEB: 'desperately sick'. Jeremiah is saying that, however well you know someone, there are some thoughts that you keep to yourself. No-one can know exactly what others are thinking. It is therefore possible to deceive even those closest to us, because the human heart is corrupted by sin; it is terminally sick – heading for death.

Only God can save us from death. He reads our thoughts and knows our condition. That is why he sent his only begotten Son to die for our sins – he knows how desperate our condition is. But 'God so loved the world that... whoever believes in him is not condemned' (John 3: 16 & 18). To trust in the Lord Jesus is our only hope of salvation.

Prayer
Lord, I know that many times my thoughts must be offensive to you. Cleanse my thoughts. Create in me a clean heart, O God, and renew a right spirit within me (Psalm 51: 10).

Today with Jeremiah

THE HOPE OF ISRAEL

Jeremiah 17: 12-13
A glorious throne, exalted from the beginning, is the place of our sanctuary. O Lord, the hope of Israel, all who forsake you will be put to shame. Those who turn away from you will be written in the dust because they have forsaken the Lord, the spring of living water.

Comment

Jeremiah's reputation in Jerusalem was that of a prophet who brought a stern, uncompromising message concerning the infidelity and immorality of the nation. The leaders, who were the shepherds of the people, were as bad as the people themselves; so, too, were the priests!

Jeremiah often thundered against the religious practices in the Temple. It may well have been supposed that he hated the Temple and had no respect for it. The reading today shows this to be untrue. He had great respect for the Temple as the very throne of God. Indeed it was because of his great respect that he abhorred the many unworthy things that happened there. The zeal of the house of the Lord consumed him.

Jeremiah looked beyond the great stone structure and elaborate furnishings of the Temple to the presence of God, symbolised in the holy of holies. This was the true significance of Israel's sanctuary. It was not the building, but the Lord himself who was 'the hope of Israel'. Those who forsook the Lord would be put to shame.

It never ceased to amaze Jeremiah that a nation so wonderfully favoured by God could turn away from him. There is no threat of judgment here; no declaration that God would punish those who turned away from him. It was unnecessary to make such threats. The consequences of turning away from God were clear and inevitable. The people who rejected God's love and protection in Judah would see disaster come as a result of their own actions. God did not have to do anything. The fate of a rebellious generation was already written in the dust of history.

The heart of the tragedy of Jerusalem was that, when the Babylonians came and laid siege to the city, many people died of thirst. Jerusalem became a 'parched place' (17: 6). Jeremiah had warned that this was the curse that comes upon those who trust in man and depend upon flesh (17: 5). But God is a 'spring of living water' – pure, cool, refreshing water – who never fails to provide for his children, for those who put their trust in him. That promise is still true today.

Prayer
Lord, help me to drink deeply from the spring of living water that you provide. Refresh me; fill me with new life. And may that new life overflow in abundance to others around me.

Today with Jeremiah

LIVING WITH UNBELIEVERS

Jeremiah 17: 14-17
Heal me, O Lord, and I shall be healed; save me and I shall be saved, for you are the one I praise. They keep saying to me, 'Where is the word of the Lord? Let it now be fulfilled!' I have not run away from being your shepherd; you know I have not desired the day of despair. What passes my lips is open before you. Do not be a terror to me; you are my refuge in the day of disaster.

Comment

This is the fourth of the personal prayers of Jeremiah recorded in the book that bears his name. Each of these prayers gives an illuminating glimpse of the man behind the message.

In these prayers we can see something of the cost of carrying a prophetic ministry. The prayers are more revealing of the character and inner thoughts of the prophet than the narratives of his activities or the record of his prophecies. It is often true that you can see more clearly into the heart of a person by listening to them pray, than by listening to their conversation.

In today's reading Jeremiah calls out to the Lord for help. He asks for healing – yet, in the light of what follows, it is doubtful if he means physical healing. Clearly he had lost his peace. He had been thoroughly disturbed by the constant verbal assault to which he had been subjected.

Since the beginning of his ministry, when as a young man he was called to be a prophet, Jeremiah had delivered messages of warning to the nation. He was well known both in Jerusalem and in the towns of Judah. Right from the beginning, his warnings had been of invasion from

Babylon – 'the boiling pot, tilting away from the north' (1: 13) – and the destruction of Jerusalem.

For thirty years Jeremiah had carried this same message. But when the Babylonians did come in 596 BC they did not destroy the city. They took some captives, but King Zedekiah was able to buy them off with gold and by stripping his palace and the Temple of treasure. The city remained unravished, contrary to Jeremiah's warnings, and life soon returned to normal. The people got on with making a living and worshipping their idols. It was another ten years (586 BC) before 'the day of disaster' took place and the Babylonians returned to sack the city.

In the meantime everyone poured scorn and heaped abuse upon the prophet. In this prayer, he took the matter before the Lord. He had been a faithful servant. He had not desired the 'day of despair' or 'day of disaster' (RSV) but being faithful as a servant of God had cost him dearly. Only God could comfort and strengthen him and restore his inner peace.

Making a good witness when you are surrounded by unbelievers – whether friends, colleagues, or even members of your own family – is not easy. The Lord knows the cost of discipleship. It is right to talk to him about our inmost feelings. He always responds, bringing healing, comfort and strength, which renews our inner peace.

Prayer
Heal me, O Lord, and I shall be healed; save me and I shall be saved, for you are the one I praise.

# THE SECOND CHANCE

Jeremiah 18: 1-4
This is the word that came to Jeremiah from the Lord: 'Go down to the potter's house, and there I will give you my message.' So I went down to the potter's house, and I saw him working at the wheel. But the pot he was shaping from the clay was marred in his hands; so the potter formed it into another pot, shaping it as seemed best to him.

Comment

This is one of the most revealing incidents in Jeremiah's ministry, and an image which is portrayed on the cover of this book. It has a lovely message. It is revealing because it shows how Jeremiah worked. His ministry was based upon his ability to listen to God, to do what he himself described as getting into 'the council of God'.

On this occasion, during one of his quiet times, he was told to go to the potter's house where he would receive God's message. There was no other instruction so he had no idea what he was to hear, or see. He was accustomed to God conveying a message to him through some incident that he witnessed or something that occurred in nature.

Jeremiah would no doubt have watched the potter carefully to note anything unusual that God might use to impress upon him and to highlight a message. It is very possible that he asked the potter what he was making and the man would have explained that he was unable to make the beautiful vase that he had in mind.

There are some pieces of clay that simply will not run, even in the hands of an experienced potter. This piece defied all the craftsman's skill. It was marred in the potter's hands.

So the man crushed it, but he did not hurl it away into the dust on his workshop floor. Instead, the potter patiently put it back on the wheel and refashioned it. The pot he made was not the one he originally intended. That might have been a thing of beauty to grace a rich man's house, but this one was probably a useful pot that might bless a busy housewife who needed sturdy kitchen utensils.

Jeremiah at once perceived the significance of the little 'parable' he had just witnessed. The Lord said to him, 'Can I not do with you as this potter does?' Sometimes we are so stubborn and we get our life into such a mess that God is not able to shape us and use us in the way that he intended or to bless us as he longs to do.

We go our own way, sometimes even with disastrous consequences, but he never abandons us. He never casts us away as worthless. If we are willing, even when we have made a mess of things, he restores us, remakes our life and gives us a second chance or even a third, or a fourth or …? He may not be able to use us as he originally intended, because those circumstances may have changed, but what he will do is to remake us and use us for his purposes. He will never cast us away.

Prayer
Lord, I want to be in your hands as the clay in the hands of the potter. Shape me as seems best to you and make be useful in your kingdom.

Today with Jeremiah

GOOD NEWS FOR NATIONS

Jeremiah 18: 6b-10
'Like clay in the hand of the potter, so are you in my hand, O house of Israel. If at any time I announce that a nation or kingdom is to be uprooted, torn down and destroyed, and if that nation I warned repents of its evil, then I will relent and not inflict on it the disaster I had planned. And if at another time I announce that a nation or kingdom is to be built up and planted, and if it does evil in my sight and does not obey me, then I will reconsider the good I had intended to do for it.'

Comment

This prophecy underlines the sovereignty of God. It states unequivocally that God is in control of the nations. In the modern world it is not an easy message for us to accept, especially as we look back at the events of the twentieth century in which there was the greatest bloodshed in history. It was a century of conflict, with its great world wars, its forty years of cold war and its record of smaller, but bitter, conflicts with fearful weapons of destruction, and increasing atrocities and terrorism. Could God really have been in control of such a violent world?

This question is not new to our generation. The same problems troubled people in Jeremiah's day. The message he received from his visit to the potter's house was a particularly powerful answer. The nations are really like clay in the potter's hands. In his hands God holds the destiny of the nations.

That does not mean to say that he directs the day to day affairs of countries. Any nation would be wonderfully blessed if they allowed God to do that! The stubbornness and spiritual blindness of mankind act as a barrier, preventing God from doing what he would like to do with the nations.

The uniqueness of this promise is that it is universally applicable to the nations. It is not just a prophecy to Israel or to those who are in a covenant relationship with God. It is a promise for any nation at any time. The key word is 'repent'. If, at any time, a nation is heading for disaster – either because God is bringing judgment upon the people or due to the inevitable consequences of their wickedness – and it heeds the warning signs and repents of its evil ways, God will turn events around to avert the disaster and to bring blessing to that nation.

Conversely, even if a nation is enjoying great prosperity, appears much favoured and is experiencing the blessings of being in a right relationship with God; if it turns away from the Lord and does evil, God will 'reconsider the good' he intended for that nation.

This is both a message of warning and of good news for nations. We cannot do evil without it affecting the whole future of the nation. There is a collective responsibility for the well being of the nation which each of its citizens must bear. We are responsible before God for exercising some influence on the nation. We should each take this promise seriously.

Prayer
Lord show me how I may rightly exercise the influence I have in my family, community and nation.

Today with Jeremiah

INNOCENT BLOOD

Jeremiah 19: 3b-5
'This is what the Lord Almighty, the God of Israel, says: Listen! I am going to bring disaster on this place that will make the ears of everyone who hears it tingle. For they have forsaken me and made this a place of foreign gods; they have burned sacrifices in it to gods that neither they nor their fathers nor the kings of Judah ever knew, and they have filled this place with the blood of the innocent. They have built the high places of Baal to burn their sons in the fire as offerings to Baal – something I did not command or mention, nor did it enter my mind.'

Comment

This prophecy is linked to one of the most dreadful episodes in the history of Israel. Idolatry had taken a grip on the nation. Once false religion or false beliefs take hold of a nation, or of individual lives, the people are driven by spiritual forces beyond their control. This is what had happened in Jerusalem, the city whose very name was linked with the God of Israel, the God whom the nation was now forsaking.

Jeremiah complained that Judah had as many gods as it had towns and that every street in Jerusalem had its own pagan shrine. It is hard to imagine how the nation came to reach such spiritual depths in so short a period. It was less than forty years since the great reformation of Josiah had cleansed the city and the towns of Judah from idolatry. His successors cared nothing about upholding his reforms; loyalty to the God of Israel meant nothing to them. They would worship any god that promised either to give the personal pleasure or political advantage that they sought.

The most detestable form of idolatrous worship was that offered to the god Molech. The sacrifices offered to him were little children, burned alive in the fire. This practice was not new. It had been introduced, according to 1 Kings 11, by King Solomon as part of his practice of setting up shrines for his foreign wives. We read that Molech was the God of the Ammonites (1 Kings 11: 7), but there is evidence to suggest that, prior to this, it originated with the Phoenicians who used a huge cauldron or pit of fire into which the babies were thrown as part of their religious ritual.

Despite Josiah having desecrated the shrine to Molech at the place called Topheth in the valley of Hinnom just south of Jerusalem, Jehoiakim revived it and the practice of child sacrifice remained popular until the destruction of the city. In this prophecy, Jeremiah does not identify the cultic practices at Topheth with Molech. It may be that many people in Jerusalem, confusing the offering of the first-born to the Lord with this detestable practice, were actually sacrificing their babies as burnt offerings to the God of Israel! Hence Jeremiah vehemently denied that such a wicked distortion of the Torah had ever even entered God's mind!

In our generation, hospitals and clinics fill black plastic-bags every day with the tiny bodies of babies wrenched from their mother's womb, to be taken to the incinerator and burned in the fire. It may be that abortion can be justified in a few exceptional circumstances, but in most instances this is surely sacrifice to the god of lust, filling the land with the blood of the innocent. How much longer can God delay bringing judgment upon us?

Prayer
Lord, have mercy.

Today with Jeremiah

THE PROPHETIC IMPERATIVE

Jeremiah 20: 8-9
Whenever I speak, I cry out proclaiming violence and destruction. So the word of the Lord has brought me insult and reproach all day long. But if I say, 'I will not mention him or speak any more in his name', his word is in my heart like a burning fire, shut up in my bones. I am weary of holding it in; indeed, I cannot.

Comment

This is another one of Jeremiah's prayer-conversations with the Lord. He began by complaining that he had been deceived and that this was why he had been 'ridiculed all day long' (v 7). In his heart he must have known that God would not deceive him, but he was really sore that the prophecies he had been given to deliver had so far not been fulfilled. This resulted in his being ridiculed, as he said, 'The word of God has brought me insult and reproach all day long'.

Jeremiah must have known at the beginning of his complaint that he was being unjust in questioning God. He certainly did not want to see disaster come upon the city he loved. His tears over the lack of response from the people to his calls for repentance were genuine. But he was surrounded by enemies who hated him and the message he declared. Even his friends were waiting for him to slip, saying, 'Perhaps he will be deceived; then we will prevail over him' (v 10).

It is small wonder that Jeremiah had days of black despair wishing he had never been called to be a prophet. Yet despite his times of depression he could never refuse to speak the word of the Lord. His call to ministry was irrevocable. He could never deny his calling and he knew that God would never deny him so long as he remained faithful.

For the prophet, the word of the Lord was the most precious thing in his life. He counted it a great privilege to be the servant of the Lord and his mouthpiece to the nation. Even though every man's hand was against him, he still could not renege on his calling. The word of the Lord was like a fire in his heart. It burned in his bones. It was more real than anything else in his life.

Jeremiah had given his whole life into God's hands and the cost was high. He had even been forbidden to marry (16: 2) and thus to enjoy the comfort of a wife and children and a settled home life. Being a prophet and proclaiming God's message had cost him dearly. But if he tried to hold back from declaring the word of the Lord he found he could not do so. Even though he knew that it would bring great trouble, that he was liable to be physically assaulted and possibly even killed, he found that he simply could not keep silent; he could not hold the word of God within him. It was like a fire burning inside him that had to be released.

It is this kind of commitment that God is looking for in each of his people. We are not all called to be prophets, but we are each called to be a witness for the living God. We are either a good witness or a bad witness.

Prayer
Lord you know the opportunities that will come today for witnessing to your truth. Help me to be a good witness.

DEALING WITH DEPRESSION

Jeremiah 20: 14, 18, 13
Cursed be the day I was born! May the day my mother bore me not be blessed! ... Why did I ever come out of the womb to see trouble and sorrow and to end my days in shame? ... Sing to the Lord! Give praise to the Lord! He rescues the life of the needy from the hands of the wicked.

Comment

Poor Jeremiah! He really did have his days of depression! When he hit a low, it was very low indeed. It is sad to think that the great prophet – who endured so much, and was so faithful to the Lord and so fearless in his public ministry – could suffer such depression in private. His public face was very different from his private face and the one he exposed to the Lord in the times he stood in his council.

This outburst, even wishing he had not been born, is part of the lengthy complaint Jeremiah took before the Lord. We were looking at some of the complaint in yesterday's reading and noted that, despite all his suffering, the prophet could not deny his calling. It was impossible for him not to declare the word of God. This shows the conflict of emotions that the prophetic ministry generated.

Jeremiah loved hearing from God; his words were his 'heart's delight' (15: 16), but they brought him trouble and sorrow from the rebellious generation among whom he was called to minister.

When you have to live and work among unbelievers there is often a high cost involved. There is a constant strain upon the emotions when you want to be accepted, or at least to live at peace with others, but your witness, by word and lifestyle, grates upon those around you.

Jeremiah did remain faithful. He did not deny God or water down the message he was given. He maintained a faithful witness right to the end of his ministry, even when he was imprisoned or put in the stocks and pelted by the public. He continued to convey the word of God to the people.

Before God, Jeremiah was often depressed. Yet in the middle of the long complaint recorded in Chapter 20, there is the little poem of praise: 'Sing to the Lord! Give praise to the Lord! He rescues the life of the needy.' This has been placed at the end of the selected verses for our reading today in order to highlight its significance.

This was how Jeremiah pulled out of depression – through praising the Lord! It may not be easy to make yourself sing a song of thanksgiving, or to read aloud one of the great psalms of praise, especially when you are feeling miserable. But it works! It takes your eyes off yourself and away from your own self-pity, misery or depressing circumstances. As you praise the Lord and lift up his name, the focus of your attention turns from yourself to him. He immediately responds with love and compassion. He dispels the depression.

Prayer
Lord, there are days when I really need your comfort as well as your compassion. Strengthen me on these difficult days and help me to praise you.

BEING FAITHFUL

Jeremiah 21: 1-4a, 5a
The word came to Jeremiah from the Lord when King Zedekiah sent to him Pashhur son of Malkijah and the priest Zephaniah son of Maaseiah. They said: 'Enquire now of the Lord for us because Nebuchadnezzar King of Babylon is attacking us. Perhaps the Lord will perform wonders for us as in times past so that he will withdraw from us.' But Jeremiah answered them, 'Tell Zedekiah, "This is what the Lord, the God of Israel, says: I am about to turn against you the weapons of war that are in your hands ... I myself will fight against you with an outstretched hand and a mighty arm."'

Comment

The book of Jeremiah, as we have it in our Bibles, does not present the record of the prophet's ministry in chronological order. This incident in Chapter 21 records an event which occurred in 588 BC in the lifetime of Zedekiah, the last King of Judah. In the following chapter (22) the narrative jumps back twenty years to the reign of Jehoahaz (or Shallum) in 608 or 609 BC. In chronological order this chapter should come between Chapters 37 and 38 (or possibly even in the middle of Chapter 37), before Jeremiah was arrested and put into prison.

The incident records a visit of the king's representatives, including the priest Zephaniah, who was also in the delegation on another similar mission (37: 3). They were sent to ask the prophet to enquire of the Lord what they should do now that the Babylonians were attacking Jerusalem.

At last Jeremiah was being consulted instead of being scorned and insulted. Here was the ideal opportunity for the prophet to gain favour with the authorities. He had only to stall and say that he would seek the Lord for guidance. The King was hoping for a miracle and praying that God would intervene as he had done in Hezekiah's day when the Assyrian army was routed outside the walls of Jerusalem. Jeremiah only had to say that he would intercede for the nation and pray for a divine intervention. Then he could have avoided prison and enjoyed a comfortable life. But he could not do so. He had to remain faithful to the mission he had been given.

Jeremiah had borne the message of warnings for nearly forty years. It had cost him family, friends, comfort and personal safety. He had sacrificed all to try to get the nation to repent and to put their trust in God – all to no avail. Now, as the hour of judgment approached, he could not renege upon his mission, even if it may cost him his life. The message he sent back to the King was uncompromising: 'If you do not obey these commands, declares the Lord, I swear by myself that this palace will become a ruin ... I will send destroyers against you' (22: 5, 7).

It was too late even for repentance. Of course, even death bed repentance can avail for eternal salvation, as Jesus promised the dying thief on the cross beside him. But that only dealt with the man's personal salvation – it did not change the circumstances he left behind. For Jerusalem, even if the King repented, it would not now change the circumstances. It was too late for that. The fate of the city was sealed.

Prayer
Lord, today I want to pray for the nation of which I am a citizen. May I be a faithful witness to your truth and a watchman among the people.

Today with Jeremiah

WHERE IS YOUR SECURITY?

Jeremiah 21: 12–13
'O House of David, this is what the Lord says:
Administer justice every morning; rescue from the hand of his oppressor the one who has been robbed, or my wrath will break out and burn like fire because of the evil you have done – burn with no-one to quench it. I am against you, Jerusalem, you who live above this valley on the rocky plateau, declares the Lord – you who say, "Who can come against us? Who can enter our refuge?"'

Comment

Jeremiah was not only concerned about the religious practices of the nation, he also watched the social and community life. Like Amos, the great eighth century prophet in Northern Israel, he took note of what was happening in every aspect of life in the nation and he took this into the council of God. Like Amos, he spread the situation before the Lord to hear his reaction and, like Amos, he learned of God's hatred of injustice and oppression. Jeremiah had thundered against these things in his Temple Sermon (Chapter 7) and now, years later, he saw the same sins as those he had warned about in the early days of his ministry.

The thing that was even more worrying for the prophet was that the people were smug and content. They were confident in the strength of Jerusalem's natural defences. The 'rocky plateau' referred to in this prophecy is most likely to have been the ancient city of David with its very steep slopes on three sides and with its mighty walls and defences that had been strengthened by successive generations.

Even back in the days when it was a Jebusite city, before David captured it and made it his capital, Jerusalem's residents had boasted that it was impregnable (2 Samuel 5: 6). Since Hezekiah had diverted the Gihon spring and 'channelled the water down the west side of the city' (2 Chronicles 32: 30), a fresh water supply was ensured which meant that Jerusalem could withstand a prolonged siege.

The leaders and the people felt secure in their fortress city, but this made them unresponsive to Jeremiah's call for repentance and deaf to his warnings of invasion from Babylon. Jeremiah knew that only the protection of God could save the city. But the blatant defiance of the principles of justice enshrined in the Torah was a deliberate breaking of the covenant, and this could only mean that God would withdraw his cover and leave the city exposed to the enemy.

We cannot deliberately turn away from the teaching of scripture and still expect to have the blessing of God upon our lives. The temptation to behave selfishly and unjustly is constantly before us. Additionally, we may find ourselves oppressing others in our relationships without even realising it. It is always a timely reminder that God hates injustice and oppression.

Prayer
Father, make me aware of any wrong attitude or behaviour that is affecting my relationship with others. Help me to set these right.

EXPLOITING OTHERS

Jeremiah 22: 15–17
'Does it make you a king to have more and more cedar? Did not your father have food and drink? He did what was right and just, so all went well with him. He defended the cause of the poor and needy, and so all went well. Is that not what it means to know me?' declares the Lord? 'But your eyes and your heart are set only on dishonest gain, on shedding innocent blood and on oppression and extortion.'

Comment

This is a strong word that Jeremiah delivered to King Jehoiakim. He was one of the sons of Josiah, but sadly he was nothing like his godly father. Josiah had been killed fighting against the Egyptians. His body had been brought back from Megiddo to Jerusalem for burial, and Jehoahaz (also known as Shallum) succeeded him. But after the Egyptians had defeated the Assyrians at Carchamish in 605 BC, they turned on Jerusalem and exacted a heavy price for Josiah's interference. They took Jehoahaz captive to Egypt and set his brother, Jehoiakim, on the throne after taking a large payment of ransom.

The new king soon set about building up the economy of the country and enhancing his own wealth and status. He was an unscrupulous man who used forced labour (v 13) and cared nothing for justice or integrity. He built himself a fine palace of the best cedar wood from Lebanon. He reopened the pagan shrines that his father had destroyed and he even reintroduced child sacrifice. He gathered around him a group of rulers and advisers for whom it was fashionable to favour Egyptian culture, including the worship of their gods. Jehoiakim cared little for the poor and his regime encouraged oppression, so that violence, extortion and murder were common place.

Jeremiah risked his life in making the pronouncement in today's reading. It was highly dangerous to criticise a ruthless monarch who was used to 'shedding innocent blood'. Jehoiakim cared nothing for the word of God or for the sanctity of the prophet who spoke in God's name. A prophet named Uriah son of Shemiah proclaimed the same message as Jeremiah concerning the fate of Jerusalem, but, unlike Jeremiah, he fled from the wrath of the king, seeking asylum in Egypt. But Jehoiakim evidently had an extradition treaty with Egypt. He brought Uriah back to Jerusalem and murdered him (Jeremiah 26: 20f).

Fearlessly, Jeremiah charged the king with being a disgrace to his father, who had carried out the great reform after the 'Book of the Law' had been found in the Temple. He reminded Jehoiakim that Josiah had always acted righteously and 'defended the cause of the poor and the needy'. It was these things which had made him a great king. Merely having a fine cedar-panelled palace was not the mark of true kingship.

It is very easy today to be captivated by material wealth – to love our fine houses, cars, computers, furniture, clothes and all the other things that money can buy. When we worship these things we become just as idolatrous as the people of Judah in Jeremiah's day.

It took a great deal of courage to tell the king that he was a greedy, evil man whose heart was set on 'dishonest gain'. But Jeremiah was impelled to speak the truth. It is often costly to speak the truth, but God never abandons his servants who speak in his name. He defends the righteous. But we do have to ensure that we speak in the right spirit, that our own hands are clean and our motives are pure.

Prayer
Lord keep me back from the sin of idolatry in the midst of a covetous generation. Help me, Father, to speak the truth at all times, but in love and righteousness.

Today with Jeremiah

FAITHFUL SHEPHERDS

Jeremiah 23: 1–3a and 4
'Woe to the shepherds who are destroying and scattering the sheep of my pasture!' declares the Lord. Therefore this is what the Lord, the God of Israel, says to the shepherds who tend my people: 'Because you have scattered my flock and driven them away and have not bestowed care on them, I will bestow punishment on you for the evil you have done', declares the Lord. 'I myself will gather the remnant of my flock out of all the countries where I have driven them ... I will place shepherds over them who will tend them, and they will no longer be afraid or terrified, nor will any be missing.'

Comment

It could be argued that Chapter 23 is the most important in the whole book of Jeremiah. It contains the heart of the prophet's message and shows something of his deep concern over the leadership of the nation, both secular and religious. The chapter opens with the words of our reading today which refers to the officials who governed the country and controlled its political and legal systems.

Usually, the term 'shepherd' is used by the prophets to refer to secular, rather than religious, leaders. They were the group of advisors and officials who formed the royal court and who administered the affairs of the nation. They levied taxes, enforced justice, conducted international diplomacy, ensured that the defences of the cities were adequate – they were generally responsible for the corporate life of the nation.

A good ruler was like a shepherd who cared for the safety and well-being of the flock. He paid special attention to those who were weak, to the young lambs, and to those who needed extra care and protection. The shepherd who ran away and deserted the flock at the first sign of danger was not a caring shepherd. Jesus used this simile to illustrate caring. Here, Jeremiah is using it in the same way. The caring shepherd is what God requires. But the behaviour of Israel's leaders was in stark contrast to the character of the 'good shepherd'.

In the previous two chapters Jeremiah had focused upon the Kings of Judah – Jehoahaz, Jehoiakim and Zedekiah – all were evil men, yet each was a son of Josiah, one of the most godly kings of Judah. In this chapter he turns from the wicked kings to the wicked rulers – the secular leaders appointed by the kings. Later in the chapter the focus shifts from the secular to the religious leaders.

Which is worse for a nation: corrupt secular leaders or corrupt religious leaders? In many ways the two are linked; for without justice a nation suffers, but without truth its foundations crumble. When the latter happens, sickness and corruption spread rapidly through the entire body. That is why Jeremiah reserves his harshest words for the priests and prophets.

In this reading, God's anger and grief at the activities and atrocities of the corrupt rulers is evident. Their actions brought suffering and tragedy to multitudes of God's people. Many had already been deported to slavery in Babylon in 597 BC, but God, who is the true Shepherd of Israel, promised to bring them back and to provide good shepherds for his people. Even in a far country, or when we simply feel distant from him, God never abandons us.

Prayer
Blessed are you, O Lord, the great Shepherd of the sheep. Thank you, Father, that you never abandon your people.

Today with Jeremiah

A RIGHTEOUS KING

Jeremiah 23: 5-6
'The days are coming', declares the Lord, 'when I will raise up to David a righteous Branch, a King who will reign wisely and do what is just and right in the land. In his days Judah will be saved and Israel will live in safety. This is the name by which he will be called: The Lord Our Righteousness.'

Comment

This is a beautiful prophecy which is repeated almost word for word in 33: 15-16. It is of great significance for the whole house of Israel as well as for Christians. It is a Messianic promise which looks forward to the coming of a righteous king. He is prophesied to come from the line of David, the king who united the tribes of Israel and established a single authority in the whole land, and, by the example of his own life, encouraged loyalty to the Lord.

The promise of a Messianic king was first given prominence in Isaiah 11 where some details of his character and mission are given. Here, the purpose of the prophecy is to give hope for the future. Jeremiah was already looking beyond the destruction of Jerusalem and the deportation and scattering of the people of Judah. He was looking towards a time of restoration when the people would once again live in safety in the land.

This is one of the promises given in the teaching of Moses and firmly rooted in the Mosaic covenant (Deuteronomy 12: 10). If the terms of the covenant were obeyed and there was faithfulness in the nation, then the Lord would allow the people to live in the land in safety. He would bestow prosperity and fruitfulness upon both the land and the people, who would eat the produce of their own labour (Leviticus 25: 18-19).

This beautiful, Messianic prophecy is given at this point in the Book of Jeremiah as a total contrast to the character of the kings in the last days of Judah before the exile. The promised Messianic king would rule wisely and 'do what is just and right in the land'. He would care for the poor and needy, unlike the greedy and self-centred 'shepherds' of Israel.

This contrast is made all the more poignant by the name of the Messianic king. He would be called 'The Lord Our Righteousness'. Everyone would have understood the point of this because Zedekiah, King of Judah, was a weak and idolatrous man, though his name, 'Zedekiah', means 'the Lord (Yahweh) is my righteousness'.

The Messianic king would be none other than the Lord of Righteousness himself. This prophecy was wonderfully fulfilled in the person of Jesus. Paul speaks of Jesus as the 'Righteousness from God'. God enables us to be justified, or made righteous, through faith in the Lord Jesus, our Messiah. Although we have all sinned and fallen short of the glory of God, we can be transformed by his grace (Romans 3: 21–24).

Prayer
Lord, we are so thankful that you have already fulfilled your promise to send a 'righteous Branch' in the coming of the Lord Jesus. We are so glad that we can have confidence in your word, that you are a faithful God who keeps his promises.

Today with Jeremiah

LIFE AFTER DEATH

Jeremiah 23: 7-8
'So then, the days are coming', declares the Lord, 'when people will no longer say, "As surely as the Lord lives, who brought the Israelites up out of Egypt", but they will say, "As surely as the Lord lives, who brought the descendants of Israel up out of the land of the north and out of all the countries where he had banished them". Then they will live in their own land.'

Comment

This passage, almost identical to 16: 14-15, is the third of the three promises given in the opening verses of Chapter 23. The first promise was that God himself would regather his scattered flock and give them faithful shepherds to tend them and care for them. The second promise was to give them a new king who would be a king of righteousness.

This third promise, which incorporates the previous two in a powerful way, speaks of restoration. Clearly it takes for granted that the tragedy of defeat, destruction of cities, captivity and exile are going to take place. This is now inevitable because the warnings had not been heeded and the sin of the nation deprived it of God's protection.

Nothing was going to stop judgment falling upon the land and great suffering coming to the people. But the prophet was now directed to look beyond the slaughter of Israel's youth and the enslavement of the people in a foreign land. This prophecy looks to the miracle that God would do in rescuing his people, in redeeming them from slavery and bringing them back to the land to begin a new life.

The prophecy remembers the greatest event in the history of Israel when God heard the cries of their ancestors who were suffering in Egypt. He had exercised his divine power and brought them out of that land, miraculously drying up the Red Sea to bring them to safety. He had fulfilled his word to restore them to the land promised to Abraham.

The prophets and teachers of Israel in every generation since the Exodus had looked back to this great saving act of God as the central event in the history of the nation. Now, Jeremiah prophesied that the day was coming when God would do something which would make the Exodus from Egypt pale into insignificance. A similar word occurs in Isaiah 43: 14-19.

Jeremiah looked forward to the day when God would overthrow the Babylonian empire and bring the people back to the land. But the prophecy has even greater significance for the inauguration of the Messianic era. It recognises that there has to be a death before there can be new life. God would allow the old Israel to die in the furnace of affliction so that a new and purified remnant could be raised up to new life. In this general sense – following, as it does, the promise of the King of Righteousness – the prophecy foreshadows the death and resurrection of Messiah. It reminds us of the new life which believers have in him and the coming of the Holy Spirit at Pentecost (harvest of first fruits).

This prophecy also has a very special and tangible relevance for today. For in our own lifetime God has been bringing the people of Israel back to the land from countries where they have been scattered for centuries. Indeed, at times, the rate of immigration has caused even secular commentators to describe it as an event of biblical proportions. More than 2,500 years after Jeremiah spoke these words of God, we are the privileged witnesses of their fulfilment.

Prayer
We rejoice that Jew and Gentile are becoming one through the redeeming work of Yeshua Ha-Mashiach. Thank you, Father, for fulfilling your promises made long ago to your people, Israel.

PERVERTED PREACHERS

Jeremiah 23: 9-11
Concerning the prophets: My heart is broken within me; all my bones tremble. I am like a drunken man, like a man overcome by wine, because of the Lord and his holy words. The land is full of adulterers; because of the curse the land lies parched and the pastures in the desert are withered. The prophets follow an evil course and use their power unjustly. 'Both prophet and priest are godless; even in my temple I find their wickedness', declares the Lord.

Comment

Jeremiah was heartbroken about the state of the land. He was fiercely patriotic and his absolute loyalty to God caused him to be in strong opposition to those who claimed to be servants of God, but whose lifestyle was a denial of their calling. Their actions were worldly, not godly. If they really had been spending time in the presence of the Lord, as their official position in the religious establishment required, then their words and deeds would have been a reflection of the word of God.

When we spend a great deal of time in the company of someone our ways become like their ways. We pick up some of their mannerisms or phrases and we reflect something of their nature and behaviour. So it is with our spiritual life. If we spend a lot of time in the presence of the Lord we become more like him. Jeremiah was using this as a criterion to judge the prophets of Judah. Their lifestyle was evil, therefore they could not have been spending time in the presence of God to hear his words and to represent him to the people.

Both prophet and priest were godless in their behaviour. They did not reflect the nature of God. His holiness and righteousness were not to be seen in their lifestyles. Their actions were evil and they used their power unjustly. Because of this a drought was afflicting the land and everywhere was parched and dry.

Jeremiah knew that when the secular leaders are wicked it causes injustice and suffering to the people. But when the preachers are wicked that spells death to the whole nation because there is no-one to proclaim the truth. There is no godly standard set in the land and therefore there is no chance of repentance and reform.

Once truth is quenched only death remains. God holds his preachers far more responsible for the state of the nation than he does the political rulers. The politicians are representatives of a party, a human institution. But the preachers are representatives of God himself.

Prayer
Lord Jesus, you who are the Way, the Truth and the Life, let your truth be so firmly embraced by your servants that it may reach out into the nation through our lives as well as through our words.

Today with Jeremiah

LIVING A LIE

Jeremiah 23: 13-14
'Among the prophets of Samaria I saw this repulsive thing: They prophesied by Baal an d led my people Israel astray. And among the prophets of Jerusalem I have seen something horrible: They commit adultery and live a lie. They strengthen the hands of evildoers, so that no-one turns from his wickedness. They are all like Sodom to me; the people of Jerusalem are like Gomorrah.'

Comment

The kingdom of Israel had already been scattered across the Assyrian Empire for 100 years. Jeremiah was using that tragedy which had befallen Judah's northern sister nation as a means of warning that a similar thing would happen in the south. He recalled Israel's fascination with Baal, the local rain god. On many occasions there had been a drought in the land, but instead of seeing it as a warning sign and repenting, the people had turned to Baal.

Now, in Judah, there was an even worse situation. Jerusalem's preachers were adulterers. The men who were charged with the responsibility for bringing the word of God to the nation were not doing so. Their whole lifestyle was a denial of their calling to be servants of God.

All Israel's prophets often used the word 'adultery' to mean 'idolatry'. For them idolatry was spiritual adultery. The nation was in a covenant relationship with God in the same way that a man was covenanted to his wife. Turning to other gods was the equivalent of a man deserting his wife – it was spiritual adultery.

In this case it is not clear in which sense Jeremiah was using the charge 'they commit adultery'. It is most likely that he meant physical adultery due to the general context of the passage.

The reference to Sodom and Gomorrah not only indicates sexual promiscuity, but probably means that both male and female prostitute shrines were to be found in the Temple, as in the days of Manasseh. These had been torn down by Josiah (2 Kings 23: 7) but reinstated by his son Jehoiakim who is said to have done 'detestable things' (2 Chronicles 35: 8).

The strongest charge Jeremiah brought against the prophets was that they strengthened the hands of evildoers. The people saw the loose lifestyle of the religious leaders and this encouraged them into even more libertarian practices.

When those who hold an office of responsibility in the Lord's service, or who are known in the community as committed believers – when they 'live a lie', they not only bring shame on the name of the Lord, they also encourage others to do evil. They become a stumbling block to the Gospel.

Prayer
Lord, help me never to live a lie. Help me to live in such a way as to bring honour and praise to your name.

FALSE PROPHETS

Jeremiah 23: 15b-16
'From the prophets of Jerusalem ungodliness has spread throughout the land.' This is what the Lord Almighty says: 'Do not listen to what the prophets are prophesying to you; they fill you with false hopes. They speak visions from their own minds, not from the mouth of the Lord.'

Comment

This continues the theme of condemning the false prophets of Jerusalem. Jeremiah had accused them of living a lie and being responsible for strengthening the hands of evildoers. Now, in this passage, he adds the charge that, because of these prophets, 'ungodliness has spread throughout the land'.

Corrupt preachers, whose lifestyle gives the lie to their teaching, do more harm than good. When the preachers who speak in the Name of God neglect to teach the truth and, additionally, fail to live according to that truth in their own lives, the whole moral character of the nation becomes corrupted.

Jeremiah was acutely aware of the international situation and the threat of a Babylonian invasion. He knew that God would not defend an unholy, unrighteous and idolatrous nation which was blatantly breaking the covenant. Yet the false prophets were teaching the exact opposite. They were reinforcing the popular belief that God would never allow Jerusalem to be captured.

This belief in the sanctity and inviolability of Jerusalem had grown since the days of Hezekiah and Isaiah when, as the result of strong intercession, God had intervened and saved the city from the Assyrians. The invading army had been routed without the defenders firing a single arrow (2 Chronicles 32: 20-21). A similar thing had happened many years earlier in the time of Jehoshaphat (2 Chronicles 20). But these were righteous kings; men of great faith, who lived godly lives. By contrast, the kings and their advisers in Jeremiah's day, were ungodly men without faith.

The most serious charge here against the official Temple prophets was that they spread complacency at the very time when they should have been sounding the alarm and calling for repentance. Jeremiah was greatly disturbed. The prophets were filling the people with false hopes. A great storm was coming and, instead of everyone getting ready to withstand it, they were lying around basking in the warm sunshine of economic prosperity and lax personal morals.

The false prophets invented visions which they relayed to the people as divinely inspired revelations from the mouth of God. They were deceiving the people and leaving them vulnerable to the enemy by their reckless actions. False prophecy is a serious sin. It misleads the people in the Name of God and brings judgment upon both the speaker and the hearers.

Prayer
Keep back your servant from presumptuous sins, O Lord. Help me both to speak the truth and to recognise the truth when I hear it.

Today with Jeremiah

STANDING IN THE COUNCIL OF GOD

Jeremiah 23: 17-18
'They keep saying to those who despise me, "The Lord says: You will have peace." And to all who follow the stubbornness of their hearts they say, "No harm will come to you". But which of them has stood in the council of the Lord to see or to hear his word? Who has listened and heard his word?'

Comment

This is the central point in Jeremiah's complaint against the false prophets: their message was wrong and they were misleading the people. It could not have been a worse time to have false prophets on the loose in the nation. It was essential that the people should be aware of the seriousness of the Babylonian threat and Jeremiah knew that there was nothing more important than hearing what God was saying about the situation.

When a nation is going through times of great difficulty, either due to internal problems or because of external threat, it is vital to hear the word of the Lord. It is at such times that men and women who regularly hear from God are the most needed and their ministries are of supreme importance.

The elders of the tribe of Issachar in King David's day were renowned for their spiritual powers of discernment. After the death of Saul the leaders of the tribes came together at Hebron 'fully determined to make David king over all Israel' (1 Chronicles 12: 38). Each of the tribes sent men ready for battle, but of Issachar it was said that its leaders were men 'who understood the times and knew what Israel should do' (v 32).

What a priceless asset they must have been to David! To have such men advising him gave him great strength and peace. At the very least, they provided confirmation of what he himself was hearing from God.

If only Josiah's sons had had such men around them to join forces with Jeremiah, the whole history of the nation would have been very different! Jerusalem might not have been destroyed. The exile may never have taken place. The suffering and slavery in Babylon might not have happened and David might still have had a descendant upon the throne.

The advisers to King Zedekiah, the last King of Judah, were not godly men: 'Which of them has stood in the council of the Lord to see or to hear his word?' asked the Lord through Jeremiah.

Learning to see what God wishes us to see, and to hear what he is wanting to communicate to us, is the most important thing in life. This is not only true for leaders, but for each one of us. Since Pentecost and the coming of the Holy Spirit upon all believers in Jesus, it is possible for each of us to hear from God. 'My sheep know me ... They listen to my voice', said Jesus John 10: 14-16).

Prayer
Lord Jesus, help me to listen more attentively so that I may recognise your voice even on busy days.

The Centre for Biblical and Hebraic Studies, also known by the Hebrew acronym Pardes, was formed in 1996 as a ministry of PWM Trust. Its aim is to enable Christians to study the Bible from an Hebraic viewpoint so that they may obtain a better understanding of its message.

This is achieved by means of residential and non-residential seminars, correspondence courses, study tours, celebrations of Jewish festivals and a range of resources including a quarterly journal, books, a bi-monthly teaching tape and other audio-tapes.

Please contact the Centre to request:
- information on the benefits of becoming a Member of the Centre
- regular news of the Centre including details of forthcoming events and new resources
- information about current correspondence courses run by the Centre
- details of the Centre's quarterly Journal
- a Centre resource catalogue
- details about the bi-monthly news and teaching tape
- information about Hebrew language tuition and resources
- a speaker to come to your area
- details of how you can help financially with the work of the Centre.

PWM Trust, incorporating PWM Team Ministries, *Prophecy Today* magazine, and the Centre for Biblical and Hebraic Studies, aims to bring the unchanging word of God to a changing world. The Trust has an international Bible teaching ministry with a particular emphasis upon the relevance of the Word of God today.

Prophecy Today is a bi-monthly magazine which examines contemporary world events from a biblical perspective. PWM produces a range of publications and tapes, promotes meetings on moral and spiritual issues and organises overseas study tours, particularly to places of biblical significance.

Please contact PWM to request:
- the quarterly PWM prayer and news letter
- a *Prophecy Today* subscription form
- a PWM resource catalogue
- details about the bi-monthly editorial update tape
- a speaker to come to your area
- details about how you can help financially with the work of PWM.

Pardes and PWM may be contacted at:

The Park, Moggerhanger, BEDFORD, MK44 3RW
Tel: (01767) 641-400 Fax: (01767) 641-515
Email: pardes@the-park.u-net.com and pwm@the-park.u-net.com